Law and Markets

Is Canada Inheriting America's Litigious Legacy?

Law and Markets

Is Canada Inheriting America's Litigious Legacy?

EDITED BY JOHN ROBSON AND OWEN LIPPERT

The Fraser Institute

Vancouver British Columbia Canada 1997

Printed in Canada.

Canadian Cataloguing in Publication Data

Main entry under title:
Law and markets

Includes bibliographical references.
ISBN 0-88975-180-3

1. Liability (Law)—Canada. 2. Actions and defenses—Canada. 3. Dispute resolution (Law)—Canada. I. Robson, John Sinclair Petifer. II. Lippert, Owen. III. Fraser Institute (Vancouver, B.C.)

KE484.L5L38 1997 346.71'022 C97-910730-X
KF450.L5L38 1997

Contents

About the Authors

DAVID E. BERNSTEIN is assistant professor at George Mason University School of Law, where he teaches Evidence and related subjects. Professor Bernstein is a graduate of Yale Law School and has served as a Research Fellow at Columbia University School of Law. He is co-editor of *Phantom Risk: Scientific Inference and the Law* (MIT Press 1993) and has written about tort reform and related issues for the *Wall Street Journal*, the *Product Safety and Liability Reporter*, the *Yale Journal of International Law*, the *Review of Litigation*, *Regulation*, and other publications.

D. GEOFFREY COWPER, Q.C., received his LL.B. from the University of British Columbia in 1980 and was admitted to the British Columbia Bar in 1982 following a one year clerkship with the Supreme Court of Canada. He practises in the area of general litigation, with an emphasis on commercial and corporate disputes, but including a variety of areas such as professional negligence, insurance law, fiduciary duty, administrative and constitutional law. Mr. Cowper has appeared before all levels of Courts in Canada and before many administrative and quasi-judicial bodies.

STEPHEN T. EASTON is professor of Economics at Simon Fraser University. He received his A.B. from Oberlin College in 1970 and an A.M. in 1972 and a Ph.D. in 1978 from the University of Chicago. He has published extensively; recent publications include *Rating Global Economic Freedom* (with Michael Walker, Fraser Institute 1992); *Education in Canada: An Analysis of Elementary, Secondary and Vocational Schooling* (Fraser Institute 1988; 2nd ed. forthcoming); *Legal Aid Efficiency: Cost and Competitiveness* (with P.J. Brantingham and P.L. Brantingham, Queen's University 1994). Professor Easton was an associate editor for *Economic Inquiry* from 1980 to 1984, on the board of editors for the *Canadian Journal of Economics* from 1984 to 1987, organizer for the

Canadian Economics Association's Canada–France Roundtable in 1988 and representative for the Canadian Economics Association to the Social Science Federation of Canada Aid to Scholarly Publications from 1991 to 1994. He is a senior research fellow of The Fraser Institute.

Bruce Feldthusen is a graduate of Queen's University (Sociology and Economics), the University of Western Ontario (Law), and University of Michigan (S.J.D.). He has been a professor of law at the University of Western Ontario since 1977, and was a visiting scholar during 1981/2 at the University of California, Berkeley and visiting professor during 1992/3 at the University of Arizona. Professor Feldthusen specializes in the law of Torts, particularly the commercial tort law governing recovery for pure economic loss; and the law of Remedies, especially personal injury compensation and punitive damages. His relevant recent publications include: *Economic Negligence* (1994); *Cases and Materials on The Law of Torts* (1996); Punitive Damages in Canada: Can The Coffee Ever be Too Hot? (1995); and, with John Palmer, Economic Analysis in the Supreme Court of Canada (1995).

Kenneth R. Foster is associate professor of Bioengineering at the University of Pennsylvania. Since the receipt of his Ph.D. in 1971, Dr. Foster has been engaged in studies related to medical uses of radio-frequency energy. In addition, he has written widely about scientific issues related to possible health risks of electromagnetic fields. He has published approximately 80 technical papers in peer-reviewed journals and numerous other articles, both in technical scientific and lay-oriented journals. He is coauthor with Peter Huber of *Phantom Risk: Scientific Inference and the Law* (MIT Press 1993) and *Judging Science* (MIT Press 1997). He is a fellow of the Institute of Electrical and Electronics Engineers (IEEE), vice chair (chair elect) of the IEEE, Engineering in Medicine and Biology Society (EMBS) Committee on Man and Radiation (COMAR), and president of the IEEE Society on Social Implications of Technology.

The Honourable **Charles Harnick** became Ontario's thirty-fifth attorney general on June 26, 1995. He is also the minister responsible for Native Affairs. Mr. Harnick was first elected member of the provincial legislative assembly for the Willowdale constituency in 1990 and acted as the Progressive Conservative's critic of the ministry of the Attorney General and the Native Affairs Secretariat, and served on the Standing Committee on the Administration of Justice during his time as a member of the opposition. In the early 1990s, he was also a member of the Select Committee on Ontario in Confederation, where he had an opportunity to increase his understanding of native and constitutional issues. After receiving his undergraduate degree in political science at York University, Mr. Harnick attended the faculty of Law at the University of Windsor. Called to the Bar in 1977, he practised civil litigation and, in 1992, was appointed a specialist in civil litigation by the Law Society of Upper Canada. Mr. Harnick is a member of the Canadian Bar Association, the Advocates Society and the Medico-Legal Society of Toronto, and has been involved with the Toronto and District Chapter of the Kidney Foundation of Canada.

RICHARD A. HAZLETON was hired by Dow Corning in 1965 and has held several positions in Process Engineering, Finance, and Manufacturing and Engineering, including assignments in Europe. He became president of Dow Corning Europe in 1991, a director of Dow Corning in 1992, president and CEO of Dow Corning in 1993, and chairman and CEO in 1994. Mr. Hazelton holds a B.S. and M.S. in chemical engineering from Purdue University, and an M.B.A. from Central Michigan University. He is also a director of the Chemical Manufacturers Association and of the Chemical Bank & Trust Company.

Mr. Hazleton became CEO of Dow Corning in the midst of the silicone breast implant controversy. Since then, he has had the opportunity to discuss his company's involvement in that issue and to publish his views on legal reform in testimony before Congress and in many forums, including the National Institute of Health's conference on biomaterials availability, a conference of the Association for Ethics in Economics, and business-school classes in crisis management. His media appearances on the issue have ranged from PBS's Frontline to the Oprah Winfrey Show.

PETER W. HUBER is a lawyer and writer. He earned a doctorate in Mechanical Engineering from MIT, and served as assistant and later associate professor at MIT for six years. He has a LL.B. from Harvard Law School and clerked on the District of Columbia

Circuit Court of Appeals for Judge Ruth Bader Ginsburg and, then, on the US Supreme Court for Justice Sandra Day O'Connor. He is a senior fellow of the Manhattan Institute for Policy Research and serves as counsel to the law firm of Kellogg, Huber, Hansen, Todd & Evans in Washington, DC.

Dr. Huber's professional expertise is in liability law and safety regulation. He writes a regular column for *Forbes* and his articles have appeared in scholarly journals (including the *Harvard Law Review* and the *Yale Law Journal*), magazines (*The New Republic, Science, Scientific American, Regulation*) and many newspapers. He has appeared on Face the Nation, the McNeil-Lehrer News Hour, and numerous other television and radio programs.

OWEN LIPPERT holds a Ph.D. in Modern European History from the University of Notre Dame, Indiana. Following his graduation in 1983, he worked as managing editor for the Asia and World Institute in Taipei, Taiwan. Returning to Canada in 1984, he worked first as a caucus researcher for the Social Credit government and, then as a policy analyst for the Office of the Premier until 1991. He joined the staff of Kim Campbell as press secretary during Campbell's tenure as attorney general of Canada and minister of Justice. In 1993, while an advisor during Campbell's leadership campaign, he taught at Carleton University and the University of British Columbia and he was a senior policy advisor in Industry and Science Canada during Campbell's tenure as Prime Minister. In 1994, Dr. Lippert worked on contract for the Canadian department of Justice before going to work as a senior policy analyst at The Fraser Institute in Vancouver, British Columbia. In 1996, he joined the Editorial Board of *The Globe & Mail* in Toronto. His specialties are public policy and legal reform.

The Honourable **ROY MCMURTRY**, after receiving an honours degree in History at the University of Toronto, took his law degree at Osgoode Hall and was called to the Ontario Bar in 1958. He practised as a trial lawyer for 17 years before election to the Ontario Legislature and appointment as attorney general of Ontario in 1975. He held this post until 1985, and was also solicitor general from 1978 to 1982. In 1985, Mr. McMurtry became Canada's high commissioner (ambassador) to Britain. Upon his return in 1988, he served as chairman and CEO of the Canadian Football League and practised law in Toronto until his appointment as associate chief justice of the Ontario Court of Justice in 1991. On February 3, 1994, following the retirement of former Chief Justice Callaghan, Mr. McMurtry was appointed the chief justice of the Ontario Court of Justice and, on February 20, 1996, he became the chief justice of Ontario.

MARK MATTSON is a litigator with experience in many forums, including the Ontario Provincial and General Division courts, the Canadian Immigration and Appeal Board, the Ontario Racing Commission, the Canadian and Ontario Parole Boards, the International Water Tribunal (Amsterdam), the Ontario Energy Board, the Environmental Assessment Board, and the Ontario Municipal Board. In recent years, the focus of his practice has been environmental law, representing public interest groups such as Environment Probe, Energy Probe, SCAT, and Probe International. In 1992, Mr. Mattson was a committee member of the Ontario Environmental Bill of Rights Advisory Group.

S. GORDON MCKEE is a partner in the litigation department at Blake, Cassels & Graydon in Toronto. He has practised exclusively in civil litigation since his call to the Ontario Bar in 1988, with emphasis on product liability, corporate commercial, professional negligence, and securities litigation, and has represented and advised various clients with respect to proceedings under the Ontario Class Proceedings Act. Mr. McKee has published articles in *Canadian Corporate Counsel, Mealey's Litigation Reports*, the *Canadian Journal of Insurance Law* and *Business and the Law*; he has also been a frequent speaker at continuing education conferences and seminars. He is a member of the Advocates Society and serves on the Advocates Society's Rules Committee. He has been a guest lecturer at the Osgoode Hall Law School Trial Advocacy Program and the Insurance Law course at York University (Osgoode Hall Law School) for a number of years.

WALTER OLSON is the author of *The Litigation Explosion* (1991), a widely discussed book on the excesses of the American legal system. He also wrote the newly published *The Excuse Factory: How Employment Law is Paralyzing the American Workplace*. He has testified before both houses of the United States Congress, spoken to the Harvard Law School and the National Press Club, and appeared on MacNeil-Lehrer, Donahue and Oprah. He is a senior fellow at the Manhattan Institute. His writings appear regularly in publications such as the *Wall Street Journal*, the *Washington Post*, the *New York Times*, the *Baltimore Sun*, *Reason*, and *Commentary*. He graduated from Yale in 1975.

SEYMOUR B. TRACHIMOVSKY is general counsel and corporate secretary of DuPont Canada. He was called to the Bar (Ontario) in 1975 after graduating from McGill University with a LL.B. in 1973. Mr. Trachimovsky received his B.Eng. (chemical) from McGill University in 1966, an M.B.A. from York University with a major in Finance in 1984, and LL.M. in tax policy from Osgoode Hall Law School in 1990. His thesis for the tax policy program was entitled Leveraged Buy-Outs and the Tax Policy Stalemate. Trachimovsky has been active in the Canadian Manufacturers Association, serving on its Board and as the chairman of its Legislation Committee. He has spoken at conferences on product liability, environmental law, competition law, and on other matters of interest to corporate counsel. Mr. Trachimovsky presently serves on the Canadian Bar Association Task Force on Civil Justice, which recently issued a report recommending significant changes to the Canadian system of justice in order to enhance access.

KONRAD VON FINCKENSTEIN was appointed the director of Investigation and Research, Competition Bureau, Industry Canada in February 1997. He received his B.A. (Hons.) in Political Science from Carleton University in 1968, was called to the bar in Ontario in 1971, and received his Q.C. in 1984.

Prior to his appointment as director of Investigation and Research, Mr. von Finckenstein was, from 1994 to 1997, the assistant deputy minister, Business Law, Industry Canada. From 1990 to 1994, he was assistant deputy attorney general, Tax Law, in the department of Justice, where he coordinated the implementation of the North American Free Trade Agreement. From 1988 to 1989, Mr. von Finckenstein was assistant deputy minister, Trade Law, in the department of Justice; from 1987 to 1988, senior general counsel, Trade Negotiations Office; from 1982 to 1986, senior general counsel, department of Regional Industrial Expansion; from 1979 to 1981, director, Commercial Law Division, in the department of Justice, and, from 1979 to 1978, legal advisor, Property and Commercial Law Section, in the department of Justice.

Craig Yirush is a Ph.D. student in American History at The Johns Hopkins University, where he is studying the political thought of the American colonies in the eighteen century. He received an M.A. (1992) and a B.A. (1990) in History from the University of British Columbia and an M.Phil. (1995) in Political Thought and Intellectual History from the University of Cambridge. He has published articles in the *Canadian Student Review, Fraser Forum,* and the St. John *Telegraph Journal.*

Since 1991, Yirush has attended many student seminars organized by The Fraser Institute, including the 1994 Student Leaders' Colloquium. In 1995, he was the Hunter Family Foundation student intern at The Fraser Institute and returned there in 1997 as the Margaret Thatcher student intern. He has received numerous awards, including a University Graduate Fellowship, University of British Columbia (1992–94); the Claude R. Lambe Fellowship, Institute of Humane Studies (1994); the Humane Studies Fellowship, Institute for Humane Studies (1996); and the Graduate Fellowship, The Johns Hopkins University (1996–97).

Law and Markets

Is Canada Inheriting America's Litigious Legacy?

Introduction

Law and Markets

John Robson and Owen Lippert

Governments function both as rule-makers and as providers of services to assist people in resolving their disputes under those rules. They must both make good rules and ensure that disputes are resolved efficiently and fairly.

When one thinks of the law and legal system, one usually thinks first of the more spectacular aspects of criminal law such as murder, rape, and arson. While instances of overt acts of aggression and the subsequent courtroom proceedings are dramatic, most legal activity involves civil cases. These are cases in which one private citizen alleges that another private citizen has failed to uphold the explicit or implicit terms of a contract. Most of us will neither deliberately burn down a restaurant nor be murdered, but we buy, sell, rent and promise almost every day.

All the laws and courts in the world will not stop disputes. Disagreements over contracts are an inevitable by-product of error, misunderstanding, larceny and the ease with which the human tendency to be more solicitous of our own rights than those of others. Civil courts and their proceedings are a necessary, desirable and, indeed, integral part of a functioning market economy.

A balance needs to be struck between the expeditious resolution of legitimate suits and the prevention or discouragement of unjustified ones: both rules of contract and of dispute settlement should be designed to this end. Particularly, the dispute resolution processes ought to aim at securing as many legitimate rights as possible, without becoming so complex and time-consuming that even a vindicated party fritters away most of what they recover prosecuting their suit.

Traditionally, the law has permitted wide latitude to parties to contract as they see fit. It imposed "reasonable person" standards in resolving disputes over whether a contract had been fulfilled, and also over what terms should be assumed to be implicitly present in a contract in areas where no explicit provisions were present. The resulting system, while not perfect, has functioned fairly well.

Over the past few decades in Canada, however, there has been an extraordinary proliferation of new legal rules and new kinds of legal rules, most of it concerned with regulatory or administrative tort law. It is time to start looking at the effect that these have had.

Rules and their enforcement

Given the impact on our lives of both statute and common law concerning private conduct and the kinds of private agreements that citizens can make, it is important to focus on developing cost-effective rules, and on making them clear. But it is no less important to create an efficient process for enforcing these rules and for settling legal disputes between private parties.

If risks and responsibilities are unfairly distributed, contracts will not be made at all. If they are not clearly stated, contracts will be made, but unnecessary disputes will arise. And if the process of dispute resolution is somehow inadequate—too slow, expensive, or arbitrary—then the benefits we ought to derive from the formal contract rights we do possess are not in fact available.

Freedom of contract is determined partly by mutual consent and partly by limitations imposed by law that may not be waived even by mutual consent. And, of course, because different jurisdictions impose different rules, those who enter into apparently identical contracts, such as manufacturers and purchasers of a particular product, can face different liability in different places. But another factor, though less obvious, is no less conclusive.

Freedom of contract is also in practice limited partly by what actually happens when a dispute arises as to the terms of a contract or their fulfilment. The performance of legal institutions matters often as much as legal rules.

How the law and the legal system influence and possibly harm the workings of the market economy is not just important; it is timely. There are, at least, anecdotal indications that something in the United States with respect to the formal rules of contract and the process of private dispute settlement has gone badly wrong. Between bad or unclear rules and inconsistent processes for resolving disputes, many distinguished American observers have concluded that there are too many lawsuits (for too much money) and too many jury awards. The results of court action are, too often, detached from the facts presented, the law, or even the scale of damages for which compensation is sought. Some Canadian observers now fear that this American malady may be incubating in Canada.

No reasonable person can fail to be alarmed at the apparent state of jurisprudence in the United States, nor at the possibility that such problems could spread to Canada. Naturally, we are not in danger of adopting the American system in its entirety, not least because it is based on very different constitutional foundations. But if America's legal problems are as bad as they seem, and if we incorporate a large number of their unwise rules and habits into our own judiciary system, then it is conceivable that we will face the same kinds of difficulties.

Structure of the book

As a result of our concern with this possibility, The Fraser Institute, together with the Manhattan Institute, convened the conference, *Law and Markets: Is Canada Inheriting America's Litigious Legacy?*, in Toronto, Canada on November 21, 1996. Experts on various aspects of this situation were invited to come and give us their views. It is our pleasure to present their papers in this volume. Though they presented a variety of views, all agreed that the daunting complexity of the topic must not deter us from a coherent investigation of it. As this is a preliminary airing of ideas, it touches on some topics while neglecting others, but our work will be well done if its impact is to persuade readers of the importance of the topic and of the need for further investigation of it.

Our first section, The American Experience, deals with what has gone wrong in the United States, both in its consequences and in its causes. In "A Canadian Litigator Looks at the American System," Canadian lawyer GEOFF COWPER recounts in detail one of the strangest and most spectacular recent American cases, in which a confused jury and tortuous legal rules combined to produce a $500 million award against a firm over a transaction whose total value was not more than $8 million. In "How America Got Its Litigation Explosion and Why Canada Should Not Consider Itself Immune," WALTER OLSON, senior fellow at the Manhattan Institute, attempts to explain which American legal rules have produced the bizarre and counterproductive results apparent in the United States today.

There are many ways in which the dispute settlement process can go awry. It can do so because a lot of rules are slightly wrong, because a few rules are very wrong, or because a lot of rules are very wrong. In "Scientific Knowledge and the American Federal Courts," Olson's colleague PETER HUBER, also a senior fellow at the Manhattan Institute, and his collaborator KENNETH FOSTER suggest that major flaws in one rule concerning scientific testimony in civil cases are responsible for much of the spectacular recent mischief. They also describe measures underway in American courts to bring this problem under control. Finally, in "Lessons from the American Experience," DAVID BERNSTEIN, professor of Law at George Mason University, suggests the lessons that Canadians can draw from the American experience, particularly about which rules to change or not to change if we seek to avoid a litigation explosion here.

In our second section, The Canadian Challenge, we ask whether such an explosion actually is already under way in Canada. Are the symptoms starting to appear, in the form of the kind of bizarre results with which Americans are all to familiar? Are we already making the kinds of rule changes that Olson and Bernstein warn us against and, if so, are they producing the results they fear? Are we moving in quite a different direction? And just how alarming are the similarities?

In "Class Actions in Canada," GORDON MCKEE of Blake, Cassels and Graydon discusses some important changes that have been made in Canadian litigation law, and expresses cautious optimism that these do not closely parallel those south of the border either in structure or in outcome.

Litigation explosions, as we have seen, can result from unwise rule changes, and such changes can have many sources. One potential source of trouble is a self-regulated legal profession trying to maximize its income through output. In "Dow Corning Breast Implant Action," the chairman of Dow Corning, RICHARD A. HAZLETON, gives an insider's view on how legal rules can create an industry ("Litigation, Inc.") devoted to launching enough lawsuits to guarantee that the attorney, if not the plaintiff, hits the jackpot. Then, in "Some Economics of the Canadian Legal Profession," economist STEPHEN T. EASTON from Simon Fraser University surveys the state of the legal profession in Canada and warns that we are now producing lawyers in Canada at a higher rate than in the United States. This contributes to the possibility that we, too, will encounter pressure from the profession to change the rules to permit more litigation.

In "Civil Liability In Canada: No Tip, No Iceberg," however, BRUCE FELDTHUSEN of the University of Western Ontario argues that what is happening in Canada has little to do with the American experience, which he also says is not nearly as extensive as anecdotal horror stories would imply. He suggests that the real problem lies with the entire system of liability itself. Its high private transaction costs, he maintains, make it an inefficient way to deter unsafe products and actions.

This brings us to the question of what we ought to be doing, either to halt an explosion if it is happening or to prevent one if it is looming. What ought we to be doing to improve the existing system even if it already works fairly well, and to anticipate future changes? In "Civil Justice Reform in Ontario," CHARLES HARNICK, attorney general for Ontario, notes a greater increase in litigation in Ontario than the machinery of justice can handle. He argues that the problem and the solution are primarily technological and administrative. More prosperity means more contracts and a faster pace of commerce, which inevitably brings more disputes over contracts and a need for their speedier resolution. The justice system has lagged behind the private sector, and must be brought up to the speed of business. Harnick also suggests one significant addition to existing rules: he champions the implementation of effective Alternative Dispute Resolution procedures in order to avoid taking many disputes to full trial. In "Is Canada Inheriting America's Litigious Legacy?" another practitioner, Ontario Chief Justice ROY MCMURTRY, an outspoken critic of delays, offers his own views on clearing up the backlog. Among the measures he suggests is that politicians and citizens must not regard the justice system as "just another social program," but should treat it—and fund it—as the foundation of good government.

As government grows larger, so too does the number of situations in which governments—essentially as private parties—confront citizens in civil proceedings. In "Canadian Economic Regulation: Balancing Efficiency and Fair Process," KONRAD VON FINCKENSTEIN, director of Investigation and Research, Competition Bureau, Industry Canada, describes some of the processes currently in place for handling such disputes both in the courts and through alternative channels. His view is that a uniquely Canadian balance between efficiency and procedural fairness has been struck, and that we should seek to refine it, rather than overthrow it.

In "An Environmental Right to Sue," MARK MATTSON, attorney for Environment Probe, suggests that not all rule changes are undesirable, even though they may increase litigation in an overburdened system. He contends that some corrective actions may deliberately or accidentally advance or retard cases in contradiction to stated public policy goals. Mattson denies that right-to-sue innovations under consideration by the federal government are as dangerous as some commentators charge. He argues that, on the contrary, these proposed changes do not go far enough.

In "Will We Be Back in Five Years? The Report of the Canadian Bar Association Task Force," SEYMOUR TRACHIMOVSKY, the general counsel for DuPont Canada, looks at the Canadian Bar Association's own study of the problems facing Canada's civil justice system. He concludes that the problem is far from under control and that in five years' time the profession will be back for another look at a problem that may, by then, be far more serious.

In the third section, The State of Canadian Judicial Statistics, our final group of authors—OWEN LIPPERT and CRAIG YIRUSH of The Fraser Institute and STEPHEN EASTON of Simon Fraser University—attempt to peer forward through the fog. In "Trends in Canadian Civil Justice," they find that visibility is severely impaired due to a lack of basic data and argue that whatever areas may require further examination, such an effort requires more complete, more reliable, and more detailed information on what is happening now.

Peering forward through the fog

This volume, drawn from our initial conference, represents the first step in an ongoing investigation. In order to look forward we need also to step back and gaze over the landscape. This will be the goal of the Fraser Institute's Law and Markets project.

Our efforts will involve examining how the law and legal system has already affected, or has the potential to affect, the efficient workings of our largely market economy. For instance, in intervening so massively in private arrangements, have governments given to the courts and to juries tasks with which they cannot cope? At one time courts and juries examined contracts and judged their fulfillment against a few clear and fundamental rules of common law. Now the judiciary increasingly must determine whether the fulfillment of contested contracts meets the conditions laid out in a voluminous and painfully obscure body of statute law and an even larger and more obscure body of regulations derived from that law. Judges and juries, many suspect, now lack the sustained expertise necessary to make consistent judgements.

Have we already reached the point prophesied by Friedrich Hayek, in which a network of legally mandated rules has become so dense and complex that regardless of their individual merits they create massive uncertainty for all, including grave uncertainty whether natural justice will be served through a transparent process? Certainly the growing tendency of legislation not to make rules, but to create and empower regulatory agencies is a sign of unmanageable complexity.

The Law and Markets project will also ask whether recent and proposed legislative changes to, for instance, securities law, may erode the efficient workings of common law principles and impair the opportunities for cooperation and contract. We will also explore the impact of very specific rules such as class action legislation or contingency fee legislation on the existing Canadian legal system. Finally, we hope to bring an economic perspective to the ever-changing world of legal rules in order to provide advice on how Canada could efficiently maximize wealth and ensure fairness in a non-coercive legal framework.

This book represents only the beginning of an examination of these and other questions. Clearly we need to know whether our laws and legal system have induced private citizens to devote more energy and resources to battles over the fulfillment of existing contracts and less to making and fulfilling mutually satisfactory ones. If they have, we need to know why. Certainly one question is whether the current dispute resolution process is becoming more of the problem and less of the solution. As we examine these questions over the next two years, we encourage others to do so as well and to share their results with us. The evidence presented in this volume makes a sufficient case that a problem exists. Serious thought is needed to understand it and to find remedies.

As always the authors have worked independently and their views do not necessarily represent the views of The Fraser Institute or of its trustees and members.

Law and Markets project

The Institute launched the Law and Markets project in the summer of 1996 in order to examine the economic consequences, current and future, of Canada's laws and legal system. The Fraser Institute has long had a strong interest in the Rule of Law and the efficiency of the legal system as critical factors in the growth of a market economy. The director of the project is Owen Lippert, a Senior Policy Analyst with the Institute since 1994. Under the aegis of the Law and Markets project, numerous articles appeared in 1996 in such publications as *The Financial Post, The Globe and Mail, Canadian Lawyer* magazine and the Sterling chain of newspapers.

In the years ahead, the Law and Markets project will begin to bring forth interesting and engaging facts and analyses from several scholars and researchers. Professors Steven Easton and Paul Brantingham of Simon Fraser University will direct the research in criminal law topics, including an update of their highly successful 1996 publication, "The Crime Bill: Who Pays." Professor Steven Globerman, also of Simon Fraser University, will direct the research on civil law topics. To provide guidance and comment, an advisory board of eminent practitioners and scholars has been formed.

The area of the law and the legal system is a rich and varied one. We look forward to contributing a much-needed economic perspective to the emerging debate over the primary ordering of Canada's economy and society.

The American Experience

A Canadian Litigator Looks at the American System

D. Geoffrey Cowper, Q.C.

A telling anecdote

Over the past 15 years as a Canadian commercial litigator, I have retained and supervised American lawyers. The most dramatic of my experiences has been my brush with the aftermath of the 500-million-dollar jury verdict in Mississippi against The Loewen Group, Inc. of Burnaby, British Columbia.

My experiences obviously do not constitute a study of this very complex and difficult area, but represent instead the views of an occasional traveller in the vast and well-populated continent of the American legal industry. The experience may be significant because in my view the prospect of the Americanization of the Canadian legal system acquired a darker tone last year with the publicity surrounding The Loewen Group's experience with an enormous adverse jury verdict in the State of Mississippi.

Parts of the story have been told in the media, so in this chapter I will present an abbreviated version and then try to draw out of that some general observations about what I believe we should be wary of in the evolution of our own system.

I should say at the beginning that I don't think this story should be considered either a typical or representative case of the American system. The outcome to the American lawyers involved was completely unexpected, and the result was, from the accounts in the media and the many American lawyers I talked to, considered entirely irrational even by American standards.

However, the potential for this kind of result, and the way in which the result flowed permits us to draw some general observations as to what some of our own goals should be in preserving parts of what have already been called the Canadian litigation culture as distinct from the American culture.

The commercial transaction

The story starts in early 1990. The Loewen Group, which is a company from Burnaby, British Columbia, has over the past ten years successfully acquired a number of funeral homes and cemeteries throughout North America, and in early 1990 it acquired a group of funeral homes in the State of Mississippi. In the process, one of the former owners, Dave Riemann, became the regional partner for The Loewen Group in Mississippi. Other acquisitions followed, including a home known as the Wright-Ferguson Home in Jackson, Mississippi. Another funeral home owner in Jackson was Jeremiah O'Keefe, who became the Plaintiff in the lawsuit. But with that acquisition the intense rivalry that previously existed between the O'Keefe and Reiman families was re-ignited.

Even here the importance of culture arises, because, for example, one of the banks of The Loewen Group at the time was the Hong Kong-Shanghai Bank. The O'Keefe home in this advertising campaign published brochures in which The Loewen Group name was present and then below it were featured the Japanese and Canadian flags, presumably because Japanese ownership of American industry was a highly emotional issue at that time. The connection between Japan and either Hong Kong or Shanghai was never obvious.

The lawsuit begins

Another thing that happened, also not uncommon in circumstances of intense commercial rivalry in the United States, was that a lawsuit was commenced. The original claim was only two or three pages long, and concerned the breach of their representation agreements to sell the plaintiff's burial insurance. The amounts of money involved in that lawsuit were comparatively trivial, in the thousands or perhaps tens of thousands of dollars. Discussions about how to bring the commercial and legal battles to an end resulted in a settlement agreement in 1991, whereby Loewen agreed to buy two of O'Keefe's funeral homes and to sell him a small funeral insurance company that it had acquired as part of their previous acquisitions in Mississippi. The matter had been settled in an acceptable way, and apparently the story had drawn to a close.

Unfortunately, the parties could not complete the settlement agreement because, among other reasons, they could not agree on price. Still, things did not appear to be too bad because O'Keefe was able almost immediately to resell the funeral homes to one of Loewen's intense competitors, apparently at a good price, and so he did not appear to have suffered a terrible economic loss as a result of that 1991 settlement agreement not closing. All that was left was a minor skirmish concerning three representation agreements for the sale of insurance; and that's when the story starts to become interesting. At this point the original complaint was amended, and became longer. Eventually it became very large; the instructions to the jury with respect to the eventual causes of action was 68 pages long.

Comment

This brings me to my first observation regarding Canadian parallels to the American situation.The various causes of action—I think you could say they flowered—and this is something that is happening in Canada.

When I went to a law school in British Columbia in the 1970s, instructions to juries charged them to decide whether there had been a breach of contract. In instructions in American cases now, juries are charged to determine whether there has been—I will exaggerate slightly to make my point—(a) a breach of contract, (b) a serious breach of contract, (c) a very serious breach of contract, (d) a really really serious breach of contract, (e) a tortious breach of contract, (f) a fraudulent breach of contract, or (g) a residual, "we're really really angry at you" breach of contract. As a result, the jury is left with very complex instructions and an opportunity to award damages for each of these various causes of action. That unfortunate situation has, to some degree, a parallel in Canada. The law in Canada—the substantive law relating to contract—has become increasingly complicated, and most of the coexistent causes of action that were present in the United States in the 1960s and 1970s have been successfully imported into Canada. This is a complex process involving changes to tort law as well as to contract law, which have indirectly led to the broadening of notions of relevant evidence. As a result, Canada now has very much the same risk of the diffusion of potential legal liability in relatively straightforward cases.

The case goes to trial

Before the O'Keefe case went to trial, the plaintiff was watching *Life Styles of the Rich and Famous,* which I haven't seen but which I'm told is a very colourful program, where he saw a lawyer featured. He thought he would add him to his legal team by reason of his obvious material success. He was a lawyer from the South known as Willis Gary, and he arrived for the trial in his personal jet which has emblazoned on it the name "Wings of Justice." This introduces another cultural factor in that lawyers in the United States often become principal players.

Willi Gary is well known. He's become even more famous, obviously, since this case, and he gives self-improvement speeches and the like. In fact, he became a celebrity in the community, a process we have seen in many other cases. Among our leading celebrities, based on the top 10 hard-cover best sellers, is Johnny Cochran, a member of O.J. Simpson's "Dream Team" of lawyers.

As noted, the plaintiff's lawsuit had modest beginnings, but one danger when you have 68 pages of jury instructions is that, as most people will tell you, juries really only want to answer one question, and so it's a struggle between the various legal teams to define that question and to get the jury to answer the question in the way that they would like to have it answered. In this case the plaintiff's focus was on the credibility of the defendant, and his lawyers succeeded in framing the whole question of the trial in those terms.

For instance, one extract from the submission of the plaintiff's counsel to the jury is: "We're trying to get you mad, somebody said that, let me tell you I want to, I want you to look me in the face and read my lips. You should be mad. You should be mad." That is not unrepresentative of the thrust of the plaintiff's submissions. His lawyer's basic focus was to get the jury angry enough at the defendant to justify, at least by emotional weight, a large jury verdict. In that he was successful.

The first verdict

Now, the next stage, which has not received much public attention in this generally very well publicized case, is that the first jury verdict which came down was for $260 million. The judge upon receiving this said essentially to the jury, "Thank you very much for answering the jury form and we'll see you tomorrow to consider the issue of punitive damages." The jury appeared troubled and a little bit puzzled, and they did so for the following reason: they handed up a note which showed that notwithstanding (or perhaps because of) the 68 pages of instructions from the judge, they'd completely misunderstood their task.

The note that was handed up by the foreman said: "We, the jury, were under the impression that we had the whole package. Our verdict was that $260 million covers both lost damages, $100 million, and punitive damages, $160 million. Our intent was to give weighted values to items 1 through 9," which sounds like an extract from an economics textbook. "In any event, the 260 was a negotiated compromise between a low of $100 million and a high of $300 million total of loss that our vote on the 260 was 10 to 2, what choices are now left open to us?"

Of course the point that they had overlooked was that they had been specifically instructed only to consider compensatory damages at that stage of the trial. The plaintiff in his submission to the jury and in the expert report had said that the loss of profit on the resale on their own calculation was less than US$1 million, and we shall see later exactly how the jury arrived at this remarkable figure of $260 million.

First let us get to the even larger final verdict. The judge asked counsel for Loewen to decide what to do with this note, and Loewen objected to the receipt of the verdict. The judge ended up holding that he would accept the $100 million, which was the lowest number on the jury form, and recharged the jury on punitive damages.

The second verdict

Many observers would say that on those facts things could not get worse. But they did. The jury went away and came back and said that they had chosen a figure of $400 million for punitive damages, giving a final verdict for a total of $500 million.

The story doesn't end there from the point of view of culture and interest, because the United States being a civilized country allows appeals. The State of Mississippi, unfortunately, requires that to obtain a stay of execution on the trial judgement, the person appealing must first post the entire amount of the verdict, plus 15 percent by way of an appeal bond, which is collateralized with cash or cash equivalent. The Loewen Group has been very successful, and is a very large company, with a market capitalization at that point in excess of $2 billion. But even a company of that size cannot readily obtain from anybody $625 million in cash; and so, between November and January of 1995, Loewen sought to obtain a ruling that it be allowed to appeal and to post a mere $125 million bond rather than the $625 million bond otherwise required.

Initially, the Mississippi Supreme Court said that a $125 million bond would be satisfactory, and a bond in that amount was posted with the Court. The Court then chose to review that ruling, and having reviewed it, decided narrowly to allow an appeal based on a $125 million bond. But then the full Court, sitting as a nine-person panel, reversed that interim ruling and required the $625 million to be posted within approximately a week. Of course that effectively compelled The Loewen Group to settle the matter, which it did, with the plaintiff and his lawyer taking settlement proceeds that can be variously valued but are in excess of $150 million.

Some lessons

What has been the aftermath and what observations should be drawn with respect to the American legal system? To answer that, let us backtrack and look at the jury form to see how the jury reached the initial figure of $260 million. The jury was asked to answer ten or twelve pages of questions dealing with various possible forms of compensatory damages: tortious, fraudulent and malicious, and so on. They set a figure for each of them, and by adding them all up they arrived at the end of these many pages at the $260 million figure. The jury would be expected to choose from among these, and instead chose them all. Clearly the instructions were too complicated, and so was the law behind them.

First lesson The explosion of the areas of liability, when in the hands of a jury, can be a dangerous thing for a litigant. It is also, in my view, a dangerous thing for society, in that the public's confidence that the jury understands what is going on declines directly with the rising degree of complexity in the law.

Second lesson The celebrity factor, which attaches to the American legal system, is dangerous. By the weight of publicity and celebrity the celebrity lawyer makes the jury believe that these matters have to be important, they have to be worth a lot of money. Why would such flamboyant and important people be involved with them if they weren't?

Third lesson Canada's restrictive approach (so far) to punitive damages is desirable. It is one that has served us well, for it is the unpredictable and potentially enormous awards for punitive damages that represent the wild cards in the American legal system. When a jury in Mississippi can award $400 million in punitive damages for a commercial transaction involving less than $8 million, one can only conclude, in my view, that punitive damages can be irrational and completely unrelated to any rational objective of the law. Unfortunately for American culture, the American Supreme Court as I read its decisions has essentially endorsed that approach to punitive damages and have recently said that there need be no connection between the amount of compensatory damages and the amount of punitive damages. Since the speech on which this article is based was delivered, the Supreme Court of the United States signalled a reversal of course in *B.M.W. of North America Inc.* v. *Gore* (U.S.S.C. May 20, 1996, #94–896) where the Court decided that a punitive award that was out of proportion to the State's legitimate goal of punishing dishonest commercial activity is unconstitutional. This ruling implicitly overrules an earlier decision, but still permits punitive awards unconnected with the size of compensatory damages.

Final lesson The appeal system, in this particular case, ended up being an additional burden instead of a safety valve, an additional obstacle rather than a help to the losing party in feeling that justice was done to its case. Any system that essentially prevents you from pursuing an appeal in those circumstances without proceeding through bankruptcy is one that deserves to be seriously criticized.

Both in Canada and the United States—and indeed elsewhere—business people naturally seek to avoid litigation. Particularly because of this one infamous case, and others like it, my clients, including The Loewen Group, have increasingly included arbitration clauses in commercial transactions in the United States. Such clauses are not unpopular with American businesses and American businessmen, first because they do not know whether they will be defendant or plaintiff in any case that may arise, and second because they understand the reluctance of anyone to do business if a minor transgression could result in an arbitrary half-billion-dollar loss. In my experience, American businessmen share many of my Canadian clients' concerns and are happy to see the customary jury system excluded from the adjudication of their complaints.

How America Got Its Litigation Explosion

Why Canada Should Not Consider Itself Immune

WALTER OLSON

It can't happen here

Many of our Canadian friends, contemplating America's disastrous experience with litigation, are inclined to say "it can't happen here." No Canadian jury, they say, would award $4.8 million to the New York mugger shot by police while trying to escape the scene. Or $2 million to the drunk who fell on the subway tracks and whose lawyer said the train should have stopped faster. Or $1 million to the would-be suicide who jumped onto the tracks on purpose—all these being actual New York cases. Canada, they say, would never have produced a case like that which caused a stir recently in my own state of Connecticut, where a man trying to escape the police in a high-speed chase crashed his motorcycle into a parked car and got not only a half-million dollars from the city of Waterbury, for having the temerity to chase him, but a hundred thousand dollars award against the owner of the parked car, on the ground it had been negligently parked in a location where it was too easy for him to run into it. Canadian culture isn't like that, they say.

The importance of culture should never be underestimated, but it is also crucial to consider something that's easier to quantify than culture, namely the rules of the game in litigation. In both the United States and Canada, these rules shape the incentives of lawyers and clients, and given a while to work, a profound change in these rules can succeed in creating a legal culture, or in turning one kind of legal culture into another. For as long as anyone can remember, Americans have maintained rules that make some kinds of lawsuits easier to file and more lucrative, especially for the lawyers, than they are in other countries, and over that whole period we've been known for having more of those sorts of lawsuits than other countries. More recently, particularly in the 1970s, we began a further and quite drastic liberalization of our rules in ways that encourage more litigation, and we indeed proceeded to get more litigation—a lot more. Canada is now being urged to adopt many of the same measures. In attempting to assess the likely result of doing so, my advice is to look south of the border and don't think it can't happen to you.

How to encourage doubtful lawsuits

The legal tradition of every great nation embodies a principle that society should discourage litigation by parties with doubtful cases. Lawsuits may sometimes be a necessary evil but they are destructive and acrimonious; they tend to paralyze life; they endanger the innocent and tempt the bully; they have a large unavoidable random factor that accounts for the proverb about going to law, "He that hath right, fears; he that hath wrong, hopes". In general they are something to be avoided except as a last resort. Not prohibited, necessarily, but discouraged.

The "loser-pays" principle

Perhaps the most important rule flowing from this principle, both practically and symbolically, is the "loser-pays" or cost indemnity idea, which holds that the losing side should be at risk for some amount payable to the opponent, an amount that's typically less than the expense inflicted on the opponent by the lawsuit in question but substantially larger than zero. The United States is the only major country whose legal system sets a price tag of essentially zero on the harm done by litigation. Someone can come up to you, dump a pile of papers on your front lawn, say terrible things about you that get printed in all the newspapers and, after you spend millions of dollars proving that each charge is untrue and after you're completely vindicated, they simply walk away. Many people will pull out their checkbook rather than face this prospect and the threat alone gives a great deal of leverage to people who want to go about picking fights on the basis of weak cases.

The rules of procedure and evidence

This terror of being sued is one that we, of course, did not invent. It was the British humorist Jerome K. Jerome who wrote:

> If a man stopped me in the street, and demanded of me my watch, I should refuse to give it to him. If he threatened to take it by force, I feel I should, though not a fighting man, do my best to protect it. If, on the other hand, he should assert his intention of trying to obtain it by means of an action in any court of law, I should take it out of my pocket and hand it to him, and think I had got off cheaply.

Although Americans may not have invented the use of a lawsuit to impose costs on an opponent, it can fairly be said that we have brought that art closest to perfection. Over the past few decades we've greatly liberalized rules of procedure, evidence and jurisdiction in ways that make it easier to dump costs on an opponent and more onerous to be sued, win or lose. Our so-called "long-arm jurisdiction" lets litigants shop around for a court that's convenient to them or hostile to their opponent. Our so-called "notice pleading" lets them get into court without specifying exactly what their opponent has done wrong or how it has hurt them, and switch theories later. And our so-called "pre-trial discovery," greatly expanded in the 1970s, allows fishing expeditions to demand the opponent's filing cabinets.

It's hard to find an area of legal procedure that the United States did *not* liberalize in recent years to make it easier to sue. We relaxed evidence rules so as to let in more dubious expert testimony when that was needed to keep a claim alive. We helped along class actions by a variety of changes that made it easier for lawyers to organize such actions for their own profit without a preliminary showing of likely success on the merits and without requiring that class members opt in. We revamped damage calculations so as to raise the rewards for suing, expanding the use of punitive and triple damages. We passed all sorts of new laws creating vague legal obligations on which people can sue—for example, workers can sue if fired without "good cause," if subjected to a "hostile work environment," or if their disabilities are not granted "reasonable accommodation."

Contingency fees

A crucial difference all along has been Americans' welcoming of the lawyers' contingency fee, which allows the lawyer to capture a share of the winnings for himself. Roman law used to ban this kind of fee, as did British law, as did the various Continental legal systems, on the grounds that it gave lawyers too sharp an incentive to overpress their cases. It was the same general principle by which it is considered a bad idea to let traffic cops keep a share of the proceeds of the tickets they hand out, or tax collectors keep a share of the assets they seize: they'll be too likely to trample the interests of those over whom they exercise force. For a long time the United States was the only major country that allowed these fees, and only in narrowly limited situations. Now we encourage them in a much wider range of situations, and unfortunately I understand that most Canadian provinces have lately also moved to legitimize the fee.

Legal culture

That trend, both in the United States and in Canada, is part of a wider relaxation of old ideas of legal ethics. Ethical rules used to discourage lawyers from "stirring up" litigation but in 1977 the United States Supreme Court decided that lawyers have a constitutional right to advertise and chase business in other ways. Justice Harry Blackmun on behalf of a five-to-four majority predicted that this would lead to an increase in litigation, but viewed this as one of the *benefits* of allowing advertising.

This series of changes to American legal rules was both cause and symptom of a great change in America's elite legal culture—by which I mean the culture of the people making the rules as opposed to the culture of the street—that is hard to overstress. American law schools by the late 1970s had stopped teaching that litigation was a destructive thing to be avoided and started teaching that it was really a good thing for society and the more of it the better. So why not deregulate the producers? Citizens were to be encouraged to seek full vindication of their legal interests, and the first step was to be fully educated as to what those interests were. By 1975, one of the most widely quoted of the new legal ethicists could write of a "professional responsibility to chase ambulances." Aggressive litigation styles were easier to rationalize if it were in the social interest to hit your opponent good and hard.

What we got, of course, was a full-fledged industry devoted to identifying chances to sue and running the resulting suits for maximum dollar output. That industry now lobbies very successfully for policies that resolve every social issue in the direction of more litigation. It is also trying to export its "products," sending emissaries to the United Kingdom, Canada and Australia, to show how it is done and how best to change the rules.

This is one of those ways in which, Quebec aside, Canada may be menaced by sharing a common language with the United States. The dominant tone of the American law reviews for the past twenty years has been extravagantly in favour of every expansion of America's litigation system, and those reviews are widely read throughout the English-speaking world, where they help spread American elite legal culture. And sure enough, the United Kingdom, Canada and Australia have all seen steps aimed at watering down the principle that the loser pays, expanding the use of contingency fees, revamping procedure in ways that encourage suing, and so forth. Continental Europe appears to be doing a better job of fending off these pressures.

It could happen in Canada

What, then, are Canadians to make of the American experience? Most importantly, if they must be influenced by American practice, they would be very well advised to listen to our current debate and not to the writings that were influential two decades ago. Back then, some very grand promises were made for litigation as a cure for social ills. But having downed the potion, we are now waking up with something worse than just a hangover: due in large measure to a change in the legal rules and to the changes in legal culture that they caused, we face an increasingly divided and embittered society, costs in the hundreds of billions of dollars, and a business and professional life where many merchants, doctors and accountants see themselves as just one unlucky jury away from losing it all. In fact, American public opinion is increasingly signalling that it considers a sign of social progress to be a court system with less needless squabbling—a court system more like Canada's, in fact.

It is doubtless frequently alleged that the Americanization of the Canadian legal system is inevitable and that Canadian lawyers, jurists and citizens may as well get used to the prospect. But it's not inevitable if the will to stop it is mustered. It is very much to be hoped that recent American innovations will be dismissed both north and south of the border as an unwise passing fad, and that a legal culture of restraint, civility, and peacemaking will turn out to have been the real wave of the future all along.

Scientific Knowledge and the American Federal Courts

KENNETH R. FOSTER AND
PETER W. HUBER[1]

If scientific, technical, or other specialized knowledge will assist the trier of fact to understand the evidence or to determine a fact in issue, a witness qualified as an expert by knowledge, skill, experience, training, or education, may testify thereto in the form of an opinion or otherwise.

—Rule 702, Federal Rules of Evidence

Conjectures that are probably wrong are of little use ... in the project of reaching a quick, final, and binding legal judgment—often of great consequence—about a particular set of events in the past. We recognize that in practice, a gatekeeping role for the judge, no matter how flexible, inevitably on occasion will prevent the jury from learning of authentic insights and innovations. That, nevertheless, is the balance that is struck by Rules of Evidence designed not for the exhaustive search for cosmic understanding but for the particularized resolution of legal disputes.

—*Daubert* v. *Merrell Dow Pharmaceuticals, Inc.*, 509 US 579, 597 (1993) (Blackmun, J., joined by White, O'Connor, Scalia, Kennedy, Souter, and Thomas, J. J.).

Notes will be found on pages 40–42.

> I do not doubt that Rule 702 confides to the judge some gatekeeping responsibility in deciding questions of the admissibility of proffered expert testimony. But I do not think it imposes on them either the obligation or the authority to become amateur scientists in order to perform that role.
>
> —*Daubert* v. *Merrell Dow Pharmaceuticals, Inc.*, 509 U.S. 579, 600-601 (1993) (Rehnquist, C.J., joined by Stevens, J., dissenting in part).

"Scientific knowledge"

What is "scientific knowledge" and when is it reliable? These deceptively simple questions have been the source of endless controversy. Whether "creation science" should be taught in schools along with the theory of evolution turns on whether creation science—or evolution, for that matter—can fairly be called "science" rather than "belief," "faith," or something else. In the courtroom, the outcome of litigation—criminal, paternity, first amendment, and civil liability cases among others—often turns on scientific evidence, the reliability of which may be hotly contested. Scientists have been arguing for years about the risks or non-risks of radon in the home, stilbestrol residues in food,[2] and other potential subtle causes of injury. Major policy disputes revolve around these issues, not least when they come to be involved in civil or criminal legal proceedings. Sometimes, as with DNA testing in capital murder trials, the reliability of a claim presented as "scientific" is a matter of life and death. And in civil suits concerning health, the reliability of a claim presented as "scientific" can be a matter of billions of dollars.

Rules of evidence are of major importance to the functioning of any legal system with respect to civil suits. One cause of America's litigation explosion is a loosening of the rules of scientific evidence, to the point where highly dubious lawsuits began to enjoy a considerable chance of success. Lately, however, things seem to be moving in a more sensible direction.

In 1993, the United States Supreme Court handed down a landmark ruling on scientific evidence, *Daubert* v. *Merrell Dow Pharmaceuticals.*[3] "Faced with a proffer of expert scientific testimony," Justice Blackmun wrote for a seven-Justice majority, "the trial judge must determine ... whether the expert is proposing to testify to (1) scientific knowledge that (2) will assist the trier of fact to understand or determine a fact in issue ... Many factors will bear on the inquiry, and we do not presume to set out a definitive checklist or test. But some general observations are appropriate."[4] The Court's "general observations" followed.

Chief Justice Rehnquist, joined by Justice Stevens, dissented. In a passage that says much about the *Daubert* controversy, the Chief Justice wrote:

> "General observations" by this Court customarily carry great weight with lower federal courts, but the ones offered here suffer from the flaw common to most such observations—they are not applied to deciding whether or not particular testimony was or was not admissible, and therefore they tend to be not only general, but vague and abstract ... Twenty-two *amicus* briefs have been filed in the case, and indeed the Court's opinion contains no less than 37 citations to *amicus* briefs and other secondary sources.
>
> The various briefs filed in this case are markedly different from typical briefs ... they deal with definitions of scientific knowledge, scientific method, scientific validity, and peer review—in short, matters far afield from the expertise of judges.[5]

The *Daubert* majority did rely on some unusual authorities. Many of its references covered familiar legal territory—law review articles, legal treatises, and the advisory notes to the Federal Rules of Evidence.[6] But the Court went much further. It cited two of the most influential philosophers of science in this century, Carl Gustav Hempel (1905–) and Sir Karl Raimund Popper (1902–1994), as well as John Ziman, a prominent physicist turned commentator on science. The High Court cited the editors of influential medical journals. It cited three *amicus* briefs filed in *Daubert* on behalf of groups of scientists, and quoted from two of them.[7] One of those groups comprised eighteen scientists, including six Nobel Laureates,[8] with expertise in chemistry, physics, meteorology, epidemiology, environmental medicine, and teratology. The second scientists' *amicus* brief had been filed on behalf of the American Association for the Advancement of Science and the National Academy of Sciences. The third group of scientists included Stephen Jay Gould, the renowned author and paleontologist.

As the Chief Justice noted in his dissent, Supreme Court opinions do not ordinarily rest on this kind of intellectual foundation. Few of the scientific sources cited by the majority would be readily at hand for most judges to consult, nor would the broader literature that those sources summarize and represent. Yet 7 Justices of the Supreme Court agreed that the meaning of a key phrase in the Federal Rules of Evidence—"scientific knowledge"—cannot be given intelligent meaning without venturing beyond the standard law library into the domains of scientists and philosophers.

Bendectin litigation

Bendectin, an effective remedy for morning sickness, was introduced in 1957 by what would later become Merrell Dow Pharmaceuticals. Eventually more than 33 million women used the drug world-wide.

Daubert v. *Merrell Dow Pharmaceuticals, Inc.,*[9] was one of more than a thousand lawsuits seeking recovery for birth defects allegedly produced by the mother's use of *Bendectin* during pregnancy.[10] Jason Daubert had been born with a rare birth defect (limb reduction) that his parents attributed to his mother's use of Bendectin during pregnancy.

In November 1989, District Court Judge Earl B. Gilliam dismissed the case on summary judgment, citing serious deficiencies in the scientific evidence proffered by the plaintiffs' expert witnesses.[11] This trial court's decision was upheld in December 1991 by the Ninth Circuit Court of Appeals, in an opinion written by Judge Alex Kozinski.[12] The United States Supreme Court then agreed to review the case.[13]

With its legal costs mushrooming, however, Merrell withdrew *Bendectin* from the market on June 9, 1983. According to the American College of Obstetrics and Gynecology, Merrell Dow's decision to discontinue the production of *Bendectin* "create[d] a significant therapeutic gap."[14] "We wouldn't bring *Bendectin* back," a Merrell spokesman declared, even "if we won every lawsuit."[15]

The science of Bendectin

The first report suggesting a link between *Bendectin* and birth defects came from Canada in 1969.[16] Other case reports and discussions about the possible teratogenic effects of the drug are scattered in the medical literature of the 1970s and 1980s. Journals noted limb deformities (limb reductions), omphalocele-gastroschisis (abnormality of the umbilicus and intestines), and neural tube defects in children born to mothers who had taken *Bendectin* or one of its various components during pregnancy.

In September 1980, responding to such reports and a request from the American College of Obstetrics and Gynecology, the (American) Federal Drug Administration's (FDA) Fertility and Maternal Health Drugs Advisory Committee reviewed the available scientific information about *Bendectin*'s association with birth defects. The FDA invited experts to share their views on whether *Bendectin* was associated with increased risk for human birth defects and, if so, whether the benefits of therapy outweighed the risks.

The committee concluded that existing data did not show an association between *Bendectin* and human birth defects. Two of 13 studies reviewed by the committee suggested a possible association, but these studies had been exploratory only and could not be taken to contradict the more focused, large-scale epidemiologic studies. The committee decided that the available studies were sufficiently large to have detected a doubling of the overall malformation rate, but not large enough to rule out a doubling of any single malformation. It therefore recommended that the FDA monitor three ongoing epidemiologic studies and limit *Bendectin* use to patients for whom nondrug morning-sickness therapies had failed.[17]

Many *Bendectin* suits were filed in the late 1970s and early 1980s. At that time, there was still some debate in the medical literature about *Bendectin*'s possible risks. A 1963 study by Bunde and Bowles[18] had found no risk, but another by Rothman in 1979 reported an odds ratio of 1.8 (nearly a doubling in risk) for congenital heart disease.[19] By the early 1990s, when *Daubert* would have come to trial, there was a much more extensive scientific record.

The literature on the human epidemiology of *Bendectin* is now voluminous. Lasagna and Shulman[20] and Brent[21] provide reviews. There have been a few statistically significant results—in the study by Golding *et al.*,[22] for example. But taken together, the results are overwhelmingly negative.

Any fair assessment of how well courts handle scientific evidence must be based on the state of science at the time of the legal proceedings. The scientific record of *Bendectin* is much more extensive today than it was in the 1970s. But it is equally true that there have been no major shifts in scientific understanding. The large scientific record available today simply confirms what most epidemiologists would have inferred from the smaller scientific record a decade or two ago: If *Bendectin* poses any risks at all, they are very small.

Frye and Daubert

Several expert witnesses appeared repeatedly for the plaintiffs in *Bendectin* litigation, including *Daubert*. One key witness was Dr. Shanna Swan,[23] a epidemiologist of high credentials working for the California Department of Health, who argued that the epidemiologic data did support the conclusion that *Bendectin* was linked with birth defects, despite the opposite conclusion reached by the authors of those same studies, and by the FDA, in its review of the overall literature. A second key witness for *Bendectin* plaintiffs was Alan K. Done.

Until 1975, most federal courts would have had little trouble excluding Dr. Swan's testimony on the basis of the "*Frye*" rule established in 1923. Under *Frye*, expert testimony was admissible only when "the thing from which the deduction is made" had been "sufficiently established to have gained general acceptance in the particular field in which it belongs."[24] Dr. Swan's plainly had not. The Ninth Circuit Court of Appeals had excluded it on that basis in the *Daubert* litigation itself, before the Supreme Court agreed to review the case.

The *Frye* rule came under attack in the 1960s and 1970s, however. Some critics viewed it as delegating legal decisions to scientists. *Frye*, they argued, imposed an unfair burden on plaintiffs. "General acceptance," they argued, had become a rubric that substituted for real analysis of the reliability and validity of proffered testimony.

The Federal Rules of Evidence, codified in 1975, are the rules of evidence that federal judges must apply. Many, though not all, state courts revised their rules along similar lines. Three Federal Rules bear directly upon scientific evidence in court:

- Rule 403 permits the exclusion of otherwise relevant evidence if its probative value is substantially outweighed by dangers of prejudice, confusion, misleading the jury, or wasting time.
- Rule 702 states that trial testimony is admissible from any qualified scientific expert who possesses "scientific, technical, or other specialized knowledge [that] will assist the trier of fact [the jury] to understand the evidence or to determine a fact in issue."
- Rule 703 provides that experts may base their opinions on data that might not be admissible as evidence, if those data

> are "reasonably relied upon by experts in the particular field in forming opinions or inferences upon the subject." This rule allows a scientific expert to rely on "hearsay evidence," which is not admitted when offered by ordinary witnesses.

For a time, some federal judges interpreted the 1975 Rules as allowing almost any testimony said to be "scientific" to go to a jury. Criticism mounted. Some critics argued that courts were issuing decisions based on pseudo-scientific testimony that had little basis in reality.[25] Some courts gradually moved back toward stricter scrutiny of scientific evidence.[26]

At issue in *Daubert* was whether the *Frye* standard had survived the codification of the Federal Rules in 1975. The Supreme Court carefully confined its discussion to scientific evidence of the kind at issue in the *Daubert* litigation itself. Rule 702 makes reference to both "scientific" and other "technical or specialized" knowledge. The latter category of evidence, which might be presented by a doctor diagnosing a specific patient, or an engineer analyzing the collapse of a bridge, is subject to *Daubert* only insofar as it implicitly or explicitly relies on more general scientific principles.[27]

All nine Justices in *Daubert* agreed that insofar as "scientific knowledge" is concerned, *Frye* had been superseded by the new Rules of Evidence. But that narrow conclusion did not define what "scientific knowledge" means. And it certainly did not determine whether "scientific knowledge" and "general acceptance" mean much the same thing, or something very different. Indeed, the Justices split seven to two on how to interpret the new "scientific knowledge" standard.

For non-legal readers, this important threshold ruling in the *Daubert* opinion is easily overlooked or misunderstood. The first—strictly legal—question before the Supreme Court was whether the drafters of the 1975 Federal Rules of Evidence had intended to incorporate *Frye* explicitly into the new Federal Rules. The Court concluded that they had not. A new phrase, "scientific knowledge," had replaced the old, "general acceptance." By analogy, the Supreme Court might conclude that the Securities Act of 1934 did not expressly incorporate prior, common-law rules that prohibited the issuance of watered stock. This would not mean that the 1934 Act therefore permitted stock-watering frauds that were previously proscribed by other statutes or common-law principles. It would simply mean that, after 1934, any such prohibitions would have to be found in the language of the new Act, rather than in the case law that it superseded.

The bulk of the *Daubert* opinion attempted to flesh out what the new term, "scientific knowledge," meant under the Federal Rules of Evidence. The seven-Justice majority affirmed that, under the 1975 Rules, federal trial judges have an important, continuing role as "gatekeepers"—a responsibility to screen testimony proffered as "scientific" rather than to admit it uncritically for consideration by the jury.[28] The *Daubert* majority stated that legal reliability depends on the scientific "reliability" of the proffered testimony.[29] There must be a logically relevant connection between the expert's reasoning and the facts at issue in a case, the reasoning must be sound, and the scientific methodology must be reliable. "Proposed testimony must be supported by appropriate validation—*i.e.*, 'good grounds,' based on what is known ... In a case involving scientific evidence, *evidentiary reliability* will be based upon *scientific validity*" (emphasis in original).[30]

The Court wrote at some length about the factors that judges should consider in their analyses under Rule 702. It directed trial judges to determine whether a theory or technique can be (or has been) tested, and whether it is "falsifi[able]."[31] "Peer review" is to be weighed as an important, though not dispositive, factor.[32] Trial judges are to consider the "known or potential rate of error" of a scientific technique and the "existence and maintenance of standards controlling the technique's operation."[33] "General acceptance" within a scientific community is an additional, important factor bearing on admissibility.[34] The Court noted that "the inquiry is a flexible one ... The focus, of course, must be solely on principles and methodology, not on the conclusions that they generate."[35]

Summing up its views in a short, concluding section, the Court wrote:

> Vigorous cross-examination, presentation of contrary evidence, and careful instruction on the burden of proof are the traditional and appropriate means of attacking shaky but admissible evidence ... These conventional devices rather than wholesale exclusion under an uncompromising "general acceptance" test, are the appropriate safeguards where the basis of scientific testimony meets the standards of Rule 702.[36]

This language is usually cited by those favouring looser standards of admissibility.[37] But the quoted sentence only reiterates that *Frye*'s focus on "general acceptance" is now replaced with *Daubert*'s focus on "valid principles." Standing alone, this single sentence from the Court's opinion simply begs the central question: how does a judge determine that scientific evidence is based on scientifically "valid principles"? How different is that inquiry, in practice, from *Frye*'s?

All we know for sure is that the High Court replaced that comparatively simple—arguably simplistic—test of *Frye* with a more nuanced and complex discussion. The relevant criteria enumerated by the *Daubert* Court centre on the "reliability" and "validity" of proffered testimony. But the meaning of "validity" when used in connection with a general scientific proposition is neither unambiguous nor uncontested among scientists themselves. What that term may mean when used in reference to any one scientific paper or study is more ambiguous still. How are judges to decide "scientific validity" when scientists and philosophers themselves cannot agree what those words mean, or when they apply?

Rules of evidence in science and law

The use of science in the courtroom raises two seemingly different—but, at a deeper level, related—issues: scientific uncertainty and misuse of science. The first arises because science often cannot provide clear-cut answers to questions that have grave implications in the courts or other branches of government. Risk assessment (the identification and quantification of risks to human health) is a notoriously imprecise science—a semi-science rather than a hard science. The data are invariably mixed; they can be interpreted to support a range of positions by the various stakeholders. Making informed decisions about risk requires the interpretation of less-than-perfect epidemiology studies, high-dose animal studies of doubtful relevance to low-dose human exposures, or other evidence. Science can identify unequivocally the cause of relatively few diseases. On the whole, science has been abysmally unsuccessful in identifying the specific causes of birth defects, cancers, and other chronic diseases that are frequently the focus of toxic tort litigation.

Important social issues must often be decided, therefore, on the basis of uncertain, ambiguous, or weak scientific evidence.

"Validity" in science is not a binary attribute, like pregnancy. Grossly invalid data or theories can usually be identified for what they are. But often decisions about validity depend on the needs one has for the data. This is not to say that "truth" is relative, as a pernicious kind of postmodernism maintains. Rather, science has limited ability to answer questions that are of great importance to people. The process of discovering scientific truth is fraught with difficulty.

The second problem, "junk science,"[38] arises when a witness seeks to present grossly fallacious interpretations of scientific data or opinions that are not supported by scientific evidence. Junk science is not a problem of science, but of science's misuse and misrepresentation to laypeople. It is a problem of the law, a consequence of the adversarial nature of legal proceedings and the difficulty that many laypeople have in evaluating technical arguments. The resulting errors need not be subtle problems in the epistemology of science. They can often be identified quite easily by any layperson who listens carefully to what the scientist-witness has to say.

In science, the ultimate test of the "validity" of a theory or data is time. Science is cumulative and, to a considerable extent, self-correcting. Scientists continually collect new data and propose new theories. Some will withstand the test of time, others will not. Bad science—grossly flawed data or theories—does not make it through peer review. Or, if it does, it becomes buried in the scientific literature, uncited and forgotten. These mechanisms are not, for obvious reasons, available in the courtroom.

Science and the law have completely different goals, which is perhaps why scientists and lawyers are so often frustrated by each other's undertakings. Science searches for cosmic understanding, and this understanding develops through a collective process that involves many scientists. The procedures and objectives of a legal trial are quite different. A trial seeks to resolve a focused legal dispute in a finite period of time.

Scientists and lawyers differ by training and, often, by temperament as well. Lawyers look for scientists who can firmly and compactly present scientific concepts to a jury of nonscientists for purposes of advocacy. But a careful scientist will often be uncomfortable with a translation that is simple and blunt enough for the lawyer's purposes. More importantly, scientists approach the question of rules of evidence quite differently from lawyers.

Scientists weigh evidence without clearly distinguishing admissible from inadmissible evidence. That distinction is very important in the law. A legal trial must make a binary and (for the litigants' purposes) utterly final choice between one side and the other. The scientific arena is, in those respects, much less demanding. The rules of evidence used by judges must be explicit, simple, and peremptory. Scientists can afford to rely on more varied, intuitive, and open-ended criteria.

When presented with evidence that is said to be "valid, reliable science," a judge must make an up-or-down call on "admissibility." The evidence either will be presented to the jury or it will not. Judges are gatekeepers. The jury has the separate, more flexible, job of "weighing" whatever evidence has been admitted. Decisions on "admissibility" may, and often do, determine the outcome of a trial, but that is beside the point. The decision that the judge makes is not, in itself, directed at the parties to litigation. It is directed at discrete packages of testimony and evidence. The issue before a judge is not whether electromagnetic fields caused this plaintiff's cancer (for example), or whether such fields ever cause cancer; the issue for the judge is whether an expert is offering sufficiently reliable, solid, trustworthy evidence that they did and do. This perspective is much more familiar to lawyers than to scientists. Scientists do not have to make two-tiered calls at the threshold before digging deeper into the evidence and forming their opinions about scientific issues.

Nor do scientists have to spend much time worrying about whether to listen to other scientists. Most scientific journals screen what they publish, but any scientist can attend a symposium and button-hole other scientists. The legal presumption is against admitting expert testimony: a litigant may not simply walk an expert into court and put him on the stand without more ado. The burden is on the party offering expert testimony to establish up front that it meets the legal criteria of admissibility—criteria like "reliability" and "validity." This is a positive responsibility for the party presenting the testimony; the party opposing it need not do anything at all. The court must be satisfied that the testimony passes muster as "scientific knowledge." If the court simply has no idea whether it does or does not, the testimony stays out.

Equally unfamiliar to many scientists is the idea that labeling evidence "inadmissible" is not the same as labeling it "false."

Judges applying the rules of evidence are not passing judgment on the ultimate truth of specific scientific propositions. They are ruling on whether a particular proposition presented by a particular witness is sufficiently reliable and well-grounded to be admissible in this trial at this point in time. Ordinary (nonscientific) witnesses are likewise forbidden to present "hearsay" testimony. The hearsay rules of evidence are not based on the (plainly incorrect) presumption that gossip is always false; gossip is quite often true. But judges concluded long ago that gossip, though sometimes true, just isn't reliable enough to be presented to a jury in court. Preliminary, unpublished, and tentatively framed scientific findings may turn out to be true too, but there is good reason to exclude evidence of this character, nevertheless. The *Daubert* Court observed that scientists often distinguish between scientific validity and reliability, but emphasized that it was using "reliability" in the sense of "evidentiary reliability—that is, trustworthiness."[39]

"Scientific validity"

The problem of distinguishing science from nonscience has been explored in depth by scientists, philosophers, and sociologists for many years.[40] The *Daubert* Court referred to three different domains of human thought: the philosophy of science, the sociology of science, and science itself.

The first of these domains, the philosophy of science, emerged as a recognizable specialty late in the nineteenth century and has roots in several major and much older philosophical traditions. In this context, the *Daubert* Court cited philosophers of science Karl Popper and Carl Hempel.[41]

The second domain, science and technology studies, brings together a much more disparate group of scholars from disciplines such as psychology, sociology, history, and philosophy. They explore how social forces influence the development of science and how scientists make decisions, exercise judgment, and make mistakes. From this field, the *Daubert* Court cited authors such as the physicist Ziman and lawyer-sociologist Sheila Jasanoff.[42]

The third domain cited by the Court is science itself. The Court referred to this body of knowledge as separate from the first two. The Court used terms like "scientific validity" and "scientific reliability," and suggested that these are separate criteria that trial judges must weigh independently.

Science offers its own perspectives on each of these subjects. The "critical rationalism" of Karl Popper emphasizes the "falsifiability" of scientific theories. According to Popper, scientific propositions must be framed in ways that make possible contradiction, if they are false; scientific theories gain authority by withstanding criticism of other scientists. This discourse is one that scientists themselves participate in. A separate, independent perspective on science, developed by cognitive psychologists (notably, Amos Tversky (1937-1996) of Stanford and Daniel Kahneman of Princeton), elucidates how people make accurate (or inaccurate) decisions under conditions of uncertainty. The Bayesian statistics behind these theories may seem esoteric, but they are certainly no more so than the writings of Hempel and Popper. These "esoteric" findings have important implications for decision making.

Conclusion: thinking and deciding

Judges plainly cannot surrender to scientists their responsibilities as gatekeepers of evidence, nor can they insist on impossibly high standards of scientific rigor. The general criteria outlined in *Daubert* are, however, similar to those that scientists themselves use to evaluate scientific evidence. They are similar to those that any intelligent layperson would use to evaluate empirical claims about the world.

The goal of science is epistemic—to achieve "cosmic understanding," as the *Daubert* majority put it.[43] The goal of the judicial process is "the particularized resolution of legal disputes."[44] The task of a judge faced with questionable scientific testimony has little to do with questions of cosmic truth; the task is to apply the Federal Rules of Evidence even-handedly, in a way that is faithful to the language of the rules and that makes sense in the very practical context of passing specific judgment on a specific claim or individual. But these rules, as interpreted in *Daubert*, involve criteria that must derive, somehow or other, from science itself.

Judges can—and will—take their best shot at an answer. That best shot will get better as lawyers and judges gain a better understanding of how science works. An old formula holds that science is close reasoning pushed up against close observation. At that level, science is not so different from the law after all.[45]

Daubert, *Frye*, and the Federal Rules of Evidence are American legal issues, but the need to judge the validity of scientific evidence in court (and in other decision-making processes) is universal. Canadians concerned about the direction that their system is taking should be interested in how American courts are grappling with these issues, and may find the trend towards more careful judicial scrutiny of proffered scientific testimony worth emulating.

Notes

1 This chapter is adapted from Kenneth R. Foster and Peter W. Huber, eds., *Judging Science: Scientific Knowledge in the Federal Courts* (MIT Press, 1997).

2 A.I. Marcus, *Cancer from Beef* (Baltimore: Johns Hopkins University Press, 1994); L. Cole, *The Politics of Radon* (AAAS Press, 1994); see K.R. Foster, D.E. Bernstein, and P.W. Huber, eds., *Phantom Risk: Scientific Inference and the Law* (Boston, MA: MIT Press, 1993), 101.

3 *Daubert* v. *Merrell Dow Pharmaceuticals, Inc.*, 509 U.S. 579 (1993).

4 *Daubert*, 509 U.S. at 592–593.

5 *Daubert*, 509 U.S. at 598–599.

6 E. Green and C. Nesson, *Problems, Cases, and Materials on Evidence* (Boston, MA: Little, Brown, 1983), 649; *Webster's Third New International Dictionary* 1252 (1986) (meaning of "scientific"); Black, *A Unified Theory of Scientific Evidence*, 56 Ford. L. Rev. 595, 599 (1988); Starrs, *Frye* v. *United States Restructured and Revitalized: A Proposal to Amend Federal Evidence Rule* 702, 26 Jurimetrics J. 249, 256 (1986); *Advisory Committee's Notes on Fed. Rule Evid.* 602; *Advisory Committee's Notes on Art. VIII of the Rules of Evidence*; 3 J. Weinstein & M. Berger, *Weinstein's Evidence* P 702[03], pp. 702–718 (1988); *ibid.*, P 702[03], pp. 702–41 to 702–42; S. Jasanoff, *The Fifth Branch: Science Advisors as Policymakers* (Cambridge, MA: Harvard University Press, 1990), 61–76; McCormick, *Scientific Evidence: Defining a New Approach to Admissibility*, 67 Iowa L. Rev. 879, 911–912 (1982); *Symposium on Science and the Rules of Evidence*, 99 F.R.D. 187, 231 (1983) (statement by Margaret Berger); Weinstein, 138 F.R.D. at 632; B. Cardozo, *The Nature of the Judcial Process* (Yale University Press, 1921), 178–9.

7 *Daubert*, 509 U.S. at 590. (citing and quoting from Brief for Nicolaas Bloembergen *et al.*, as Amici Curiae 9); ibid. (citing and quoting fm Brief for American Association for the Advancement of Science and the National Academy of Sciences as Amici Curiae 7-8); id. at 2798 (citing Brief for Ronald Bayer et al. as Amici Curiae).

8 Nicolaas Bloembergen in Physics, 1981; Dudley R. Herschbach, in Chemistry, 1986; Jerome Karle, in Chemistry, 1985; Wassily Leontief, in Economics, 1973; William N. Lipscomb, in Chemistry, 1976; Arno A. Penzias, in Physics, 1978.
9 727 F. Supp. 570 (S.D. Cal. 1989),aff'd, 951 F.2d 1128 (9th Cir. 1991), vacated and remanded, 509 U.S. 579 (1993), aff'd 43 F. 3d 1311 (9th Cir. 1995), cert. denied, 116 S. Ct. 189 (1995).
10 See K.R. Foster, D.E. Bernstein, and P. W. Huber, eds., *Phantom Risk: Scientific Inference and the Law* (Boston: MIT Press, 1993).
11 *Daubert* v. *Merrell Dow Pharmaceuticals, Inc.*, 727 F. Supp. 570 (S.D. Cal. 1989).
12 *Daubert* v. *Merrell Dow Pharmaceuticals, Inc.*, 951 F.2d 1128 (9th Cir. 1991).
13 *Daubert* v. *Merrell Dow Pharmaceuticals, Inc.*, 506 U.S. 914 (1993).
14 Board of Trustees of the American Medical Association, *Impact of Product Liability on the Development of New Medical Technologies*, Report A-88, Resolution 6, A-87 (1988), 11.
15 Quoted in C. Skrzycki, The Risky Business of Birth Control, U.S. News & World Report, May 26, 1986, 42.
16 D.C. Paterson, *Congenital Deformities*, 101 Can. Med. Assn. J. 175–176 (1969).
17 Public Health Service, *Hearing before the Fertility and Maternal Health Drugs Advisory Committee, Department of Health and Human Services, Public Health Service, Food and Drug Administration* (Washington, DC: Government Printing Office, 1990).
18 C.A. Bunde and D.M. Bowles, *A Technique for Controlled Survey of Case Records*, 5 Curr. Ther. Res. 245-8 (1963).
19 K.J. Rothman *et al.*, *Exogenous Hormones and Other Drug Exposures of Children with Congenital Heart Disease*, 109 Am. J. Epidemiol. 433–9 (1979).
20 L. Lasagna and S.R. Shulman, Bendectin and Causation, in K.R. Foster, D.E. Bernstein, and P.W. Huber, eds., *Phantom Risk: Scientific Inference and the Law* (Boston: MIT Press, 1993), 101.
21 R.L. Brent, *Bendectin: Review of the Medical Literature of a Comprehensively Studied Human Nonteratogen and the Most Prevalent Tortogen-litogen*, 9 Reprod. Toxic. 337–349 (1995).
22 J. Golding, S.P. Vivian, and J.A. Baldwin, *Maternal Anti-Nauseants and Clefts of Lip and Palate*, 2 Hum. Toxicol. 63-73 (1983).
23 Dr. Swan is currently providing expert testimony for plaintiffs in breast implant litigation.
24 *Frye* v. *United States*, 293F. 1013, 1014 (D.C. Cir. 1923).
25 See generally K.R. Foster, D.E. Bernstein, and P.W. Huber, eds., *Phantom Risk: Scientific Inference and the Law* (Boston: MIT Press, 1993); P.W. Huber, *Galileo's Revenge: Junk Science in the Courtroom*

(New York: Basic Books, 1991). One notorious case was *Wells* v. *Ortho Pharmaceutical Corp.*, 615 F. Supp. 262 (N.D. Ga. 1985), which resulted in a $4.7 million award for birth defects allegedly resulting from the mother's use of spermicide (K.R. Foster, D.E. Bernstein, and P.W. Huber, eds., *Phantom Risk: Scientific Inference and the Law* (Boston: MIT Press, 1993), 137–138.

26 For example, *Christopherson* v. *Allied Signal Corp.*, 939 F 2d 1106 (5th Cir. 1991) (en banc).

27 A physician who testifies that (s)he relied on a standard laboratory test to diagnose disease in a specific patient is presenting some pure science and some applied knowledge. The scientific proposition is that a Test A is a reliable, valid, indicator of Disease X. The technical half of the testimony involves the specific application of the test to a specific patient. "Our discussion is limited to the scientific context," the *Daubert* majority stated, "because that is the nature of the expertise offered here." *Daubert*, 113 S. Ct. at 2795 n.8.

28 *Daubert*, 509 U.S. at 597.

29 *Daubert*, 509 U.S. at 590.

30 *Daubert*, 509 U.S. at 590 and n.9.

31 *Daubert*, 509 U.S. at 593.

32 *Daubert*, 509 U.S. at 594.

33 *Daubert*, 509 U.S. at 593.

34 *Daubert*, 509 U.S. at 594 (citing *United States* v. *Downing*, 753 F2d 1224, 1238 (3d Cir. 1985)).

35 *Daubert*, 509 U.S. at 594–595.

36 *Daubert*, 509 U.S. at 596.

37 See K. Chesebro, Taking *Daubert*'s Focus Seriously: The Methodology/Conclusion Distinction, 15 Cardozo L. Rev. 1745 (1994).

38 P.W. Huber, *Galileo's Revenge: Junk Science in the Courtroom* (New York: Basic Books, 1991).

39 *Daubert*, 509 U.S. at 591 n.9.

40 An interesting and accessible discussion for laypeople, is A.F. Chalmers, *What Is This Thing Called Science*, 2d ed. (Indianapolis: Hackett, 1982).

41 *Daubert*, 509 U.S. at 593–594.

42 *Daubert*, 509 U.S. at 593–594.

43 *Daubert*, 509 U.S. at 597.

44 *Daubert*, 509 U.S. at 597.

45 H. Margolis, *Paradigms and Barriers: How Habits of the Mind Govern Scientific Beliefs* (Chicago: Chicago University Press, 1993), 178.

Lessons from the American Experience

DAVID E. BERNSTEIN

Symptoms and solutions

Is Canada inheriting America's litigious legacy? On the face of it, the question seems alarmist, if not absurd. The relative volume of Canadian civil litigation is still well below America's, and the Canadian legal culture has not deteriorated to anything approaching the American legal culture's dismal state.

Nevertheless, there are reasons to be concerned. Craig Yirush of The Fraser Institute has found that the cost of medical malpractice suits in Canada has jumped 338 percent over the last ten years.[1] Even worse, liability premiums for auditors have gone up tenfold in the last seven years.[2]

Meanwhile, recent reforms allowing class actions and limited contingency fees in Ontario and British Columbia have sparked concern that the restraint that has characterized Canadian legal culture may soon break down, and several more obscure changes in Canadian law and procedure may also threaten to take Canada in a highly undesirable direction.

Canada has not yet gone past the point of no return. If it is to avoid replicating the American experience, Canadians must

Notes will be found on pages 49–50.

learn lessons from the United States. There are three such lessons that deserve particular attention:

- if Canadians wish to increase access to their civil justice system, they should consider adopting the British conditional fee system rather than the American contingency fee system
- the Canadian legal system should continue to use civil juries only rarely, if at all, particularly in tort cases
- the burden of proof should remain on plaintiffs in tort cases.

Canadians should consider adopting the British conditional fee system rather than the American contingency fee system

In Canada, as in other common-law countries, there is pressure from both within and without the legal system to increase the use of contingency fees in order to promote access to justice among the poor and middle class who cannot afford standard hourly fees. This position has merit, but it is important to adopt the right sort of fee system.

The American contingency fee system Under the American *contingency fee* system, a plaintiff's lawyer takes no money up front but gets paid a percentage of any recovery of damages. Typically, the lawyer takes 33 to 40 percent of any award, after deducting expenses. The biggest problem with this system is that it encourages speculative litigation. One can define a speculative claim as one whose success depends not on the intrinsic legal merits of the claim but on fortuity.

Breast implant litigation in the United States is an example of speculative litigation. The plaintiffs have never had any valid scientific evidence on their side, and they have actually lost the vast majority of cases. Nevertheless, plaintiffs' attorneys continue to bring these cases because they win an occasional large verdict from a sympathetic or credulous jury.[3]

Contingency fees, in combination with the unique and pernicious absence of a "loser-pays" rule in the United States, encourage such speculative litigation because a plaintiff can bring a claim without any financial risk, while his attorney, by spreading risk among many speculative claims, can be almost assured of adequate overall compensation because the occasional victories he wins bring substantial contingency fees.

This arrangement is to be avoided. Contingency fees do have a major advantage in that they increase access to civil justice. Canada, however, would do much better to adopt the United Kingdom's *conditional fee* system instead of the United States' contingency fee system.

The British conditional fee system In the United Kingdom, attorneys may now enter into a fee agreement with plaintiffs that provides no fee if the claim is unsuccessful, but allows the attorney to collect up to double his normal fee if the plaintiff recovers damages. British lawyers have taken to calling these fees "conditional fees" to distinguish them from American-style contingency fees, which remain banned.[4]

With an allowable fee uplift of 100 percent (in other words, double the normal fee), British lawyers have an incentive to take any case on a conditional-fee basis that has a greater than 50 percent chance of, at the very least, leading to a settlement. The British conditional fee system therefore discourages speculative litigation while still enhancing access to the courts for plaintiffs with solid claims.[5]

The Canadian legal system should continue to use civil juries rarely, if at all, particularly for tort cases

As has been true for several decades, Canadian tort cases are typically heard by judges alone, not juries.[6] However, the trend seems to be in favour of more jury trials. For example, in the past, Canadian judges would routinely deny jury trials in medical malpractice cases if the defendant opposed using a jury. This is no longer the case.[7] So far, Canadian plaintiffs' attorneys still seek jury trials only rarely. This, however, may change, as attorneys recognize the advantages jury trials bring to plaintiffs.

Meanwhile, various commentators in the United States have begun to question seriously the role of juries in deciding civil cases, particularly complex tort cases.[8] There are three major reasons for the current skepticism about juries.

First, juries undermine certainty. Juries do not and cannot officially explain the reasons for their decisions, so their verdicts have no precedential value. Nor are juries bound by judicial opinions rejecting prior claims based on the same evidence. Plaintiffs' attorneys in the United States therefore find that playing the litigation lottery is profitable: they bring the same dubious multimillion dollar claim before many juries in the expectation that a few random victories will more than compensate for a larger number of losses. In contrast, in Canada and other common-law countries that do not generally use civil juries, if a judge issues an opinion rejecting a particular factual claim the claim tends to die out because other judges follow the precedent.[9]

Second, lay juries deciding complex cases frequently do not comprehend the evidence put before them.[10] Indeed, American trial lawyers often use their peremptory challenges to strike any potential juror who may have some expertise regarding the issue before the court, and some lawyers will even try to exclude educated members of the jury pool across the board. This factor adds significantly to the possibility that a plaintiff will emerge victorious in a meritless case.

Third, even when jurors understand the evidence put before them, they do not necessarily pay attention to it. They might sympathize with the injured plaintiffs, or desire to punish the defendants, and therefore decide to ignore the evidence. Because they do not have to explain the reasons for their decisions, juries can get away with this much more easily than judges.

Occasionally, when juries slip up, their prejudices are revealed and judges overturn their verdicts. This occurred, for example, in a personal injury trial against defendants who had spilled the chemical dioxin in a nearby community. The jurors awarded the plaintiffs only $1 in actual damages, which means that they (correctly) found that dioxin was not likely the cause of plaintiffs' assorted injuries. But the jurors went on to award $16 million in punitive damages. This award was so clearly disproportionate that the court of appeals overturned it.[11] However, had the jury structured its award so that the plaintiffs received $8 million in compensatory damages and $8 million in punitives, the award would probably have been upheld.

Unfortunately, in the United States there is a constitutional right to a trial by jury, so reforms have only come at the margins, such as by putting responsibility for punitive damages solely in the hands of judges. Canada, however, has no reason to follow the American example and increase its use of juries.

The burden of proof should remain on plaintiffs in tort cases.

That the burden of proof rests with the plaintiff in civil cases is as fundamental to our conception of justice as is the presumption of innocence in criminal cases. But, in American tort cases involving "hot-button" issues it has been significantly undermined. In the early 1980s, lawsuits alleging harm from environmental pollutants and pharmaceutical products became increasingly common in the United States. Many commentators argued that in such cases, courts should shift the burden of proof to the defendants to prove that they did not cause the plaintiff's injury.[12]

Worse, some courts actually adopted this theory explicitly, at least when there was proof of defendant's negligence. In *Allen* v. *United States*, for example, a 1984 case involving exposure to nuclear radiation, a federal district court held that once the plaintiff showed that the defendant was negligent, the jury was entitled to find causation "absent persuasive proof to the contrary offered by the defendant."[13] More often, courts, and particularly juries, subtly and implicitly shifted the burden of proof to defendants.

In my view, the debate over the rules of evidence, described by Kenneth Foster and Peter Huber in another contribution to this volume, was actually part of this larger debate over whether plaintiffs should retain the burden of proof in toxic tort cases. By forcing plaintiffs to present scientifically valid evidence, and encouraging courts to grant summary judgment when that evidence is not legally sufficient, the United States Supreme Court's 1993 *Daubert* decision has now firmly placed the burden of proof on plaintiffs. Junk science, in turn, is on the defensive. Because most Canadian tort cases are heard by judges, the Rules of Evidence really don't come into play in toxic tort cases in Canada. When functioning as gatekeepers for a jury, judges admit some testimony and exclude some, whereas when sitting in judgement alone they simply disregard whatever they would not have allowed a jury to hear.

But there is still the danger that Canadian courts might start explicitly placing the burden of proof on defendants, and indeed there is some evidence that this is happening. In *Snell* v. *Farrell*,[14] a 1991 medical malpractice case, the Canadian Supreme Court held that the burden lay on the plaintiff to show that the defendant's negligence had caused her loss. However, the court held that the burden was satisfied in this case despite the fact that the plaintiff's medical witness refused to testify that the defendant's negligence caused the injury. According to the court, the plaintiff's evidence was sufficient because it supported an inference of causation based on "common sense."

If we take this opinion literally, it is very dangerous. It seems to hold that once a plaintiff shows that the defendant was negligent, and brings in any evidence of causation, even purely temporal, the burden shifts to the defendant to disprove the plaintiff's claim of injury. Justice Sopinka, for the court, denied rather uncomfortably that he was shifting the burden of proof.

> It is not strictly accurate to speak of the burden shifting to the defendant when what is meant is that evidence adduced by the plaintiff may result in an inference being drawn adverse to the defendant. Whether an inference is or is not drawn is a matter of weighing evidence. The defendant runs the risk of an adverse inference in the absence of evidence to the contrary.

Looking at that statement in the context of what the court ultimately held in *Snell,* if a plaintiff presents "common sense" evidence in a medical malpractice case, an "adverse inference" can be drawn against a defendant. That sounds a lot like burden-shifting. The court's uneasy justification, meanwhile, suggests that it is prepared to engage in and rationalize at least some such shifting. Thus the Canadian Supreme Court's opinion in *Snell* could ultimately lead to an avalanche of junk science in Canadian courtrooms. How *Snell* will ultimately play out remains to be seen, but it is something to be very wary of.

Conclusion: three rule changes to avoid

So, to conclude, three lurking dangers to Canada's civil justice system deserve particular attention. The first danger is American-style contingency fees; the second is increased use of civil juries; and the third is the subtle or explicit shifting of the burden of proof to defendants in tort cases. To be sure, regardless of what happens with each of those issues, the Canadian legal system has certain advantages that appear unlikely to be done away with anytime soon, including the loser-pays rules, caps on non-pecuniary damages in tort cases, and limited punitive damages.

Canadians cannot, however, afford to be complacent. It took only a few short decades for the American civil justice system to decline, and it may never recover. Given Canada's smaller size, and the American example at hand, decline could come even more swiftly in Canada.

Notes

1 The Canadian Medical Protective Association, personal communication with Craig Yirush, 1996. Cited by Neville Nankivell, Alarm Bells Ringing Over Perceived Crisis in Civil Justice System, *Financial Post*, November 9, 1996: 23.
2 The Canadian Institute for Chartered Accountants, personal communication with Craig Yirush, 1996. Cited *ibid.*
3 See David E. Bernstein, *Breast Implants: A Study in Phantom Risks*, Manhattan Institute Research Memorandum No. 5, April 1995.
4 See, e.g., Peter Parke Says "No Win No Fee" Will Not Follow the US Example, *The Lawyer*, June 20, 1995: 10.
5 Barjinder Sahota, Exploding the Myths of Conditional Fees, 145 New Law Journal 592 (1995).
6 Joan M. Gilmour, Overview of Medical Malpractice Law in Canada, 3 Annals of Health Law 179, 184 (1994). Unfortunately, it seems impossible to get statistics regarding exactly what percentage of Canadian civil cases are heard by juries.
7 *Ibid.*
8 E.g., George Priest, Justifying the Civil Jury, in Robert E. Litan, ed., *Verdict: Assissing the Civil Jury System*: 103 (Washington, D.C. 1993).
9 For example, in *Rothwell* v. *Raes*, 76 D.L.R. 4th 280 (Ont. Ct. App. 1990), the court upheld the trial court's decision favouring the defendant in a case alleging brain damage from Pertussis, a vaccine. The court held that the mere possibility that the vaccine caused an injury does not amount to the probability necessary to sustain a plaintiff's verdict. Similarly, an English court rejected a claim linking Pertussis vaccine to brain damage in 1988. *Loveday* v. *Renton*, 1 Med. L.R. 121, *The Times*, March 31, 1988 (March 20, 1991) (available on LEXIS, Enggen file); see D. Hull, Pædiatrics, in *A Practical Guide to Medicine and the Law* 199, 207 (J. P. Jackson ed., 1991). Unlike in the United States, where attorneys would have forum-shopped for more sympathetic jurisdictions, the prodefendant decisions in these cases essentially halted vaccine litigation in Canada and England. In England, legal aid refused for a time to support further such claims. See Simon Pearl, Vaccine Litigation, *L. Soc'y's Gazette*, April 15, 1989: 6.

10 E.g., Special Committee on Jury Comprehension of the ABA Section of Litigation, Jury Comprehension in Complex Cases (1989). (See also Foster and Huber, this volume.)

11 *Kemner* v. *Monsanto*, 217 Ill. App. 3d, 160 Ill. Dec. 192, 576 N.E.2d 1146, *appeal denied*, 142 Ill.2d 655, 164 Ill. Dec. 918, 584 S.E.2d 1301 (1991).

12 E.g., Thomas W. Henderson, Toxic Tort Litigation: Medical and Scientific Principles in Causation, 132 *Am. J. Epidemiology* S69 (1990).

13 *Allen* v. *U.S.*, 588 F. Supp. 247, 415 (1984).

14 [1990] 2 S.C.R. 311.

The Canadian Challenge

Class Actions in Canada

A Potentially Momentous Change to Canadian Litigation

S. Gordon McKee

A potentially momentous—and potentially very troublesome—change in the procedural rules for lawsuits in Canada concerns the conditions under which class action suits will be permitted, if permitted at all. Until 1993, class actions were not permitted in Canada except in the province of Quebec, the only civil law jurisdiction in Canada. However, legislation allowing class actions has been recently enacted in the provinces of Ontario and British Columbia, and it remains to be seen whether the other provinces and territories will follow suit.

Strong social arguments were made by proponents of class action legislation that it will permit the pursuit of meritorious claims that individually would be uneconomical to pursue, it will deter potential defendants from wrongful conduct and it will reduce the cost of judicial resources required to resolve disputes. As in many other jurisdictions, provincial governments in Canada have focused more recently on ways to increase ac-

---

Notes will be found on page 66.

cess to justice but at the same time reduce the burden on the public purse. The Ontario and British Columbia legislatures have accepted that class actions will help to accomplish both of these goals.

When class action reform was contemplated in Ontario, however, many argued that it would result in a large number of frivolous and abusive lawsuits, as was perceived to have happened in the United States. Further, strong arguments were made against class action legislation, most notably because of the substantial unfairness to defendants involved in this type of litigation and because complex multi-jurisdictional class action suits may in fact be a greater burden on judicial resources than multiple individual claims. But for the notice that is required to be sent to all plaintiff class members as part of the class action procedure, many of them will never initiate proceedings, often because they will not otherwise believe they have a claim with any merit, they are not aware of their ability to make a claim, their damages are not sufficiently large to warrant the expense or inconvenience of pursuing a claim or they are not aware of or do not believe there is any causal link between the defendants and their injury or loss. Class action legislation generally permits the plaintiff class lawyer to notify all class members of the proceedings where, but for the legislation, that lawyer would not be permitted to solicit professional employment from the class members to represent them in individual claims. Accordingly, class action legislation can result in massive and complex actions that are expensive to all involved and a significant burden on judicial resources, where only a few relatively simple actions by individual plaintiffs would have otherwise existed. Furthermore, as the number of plaintiffs increases through the class action process, it becomes increasingly difficult for defendants to estimate the size of the potential damage awards and their exposure, at least in part because the defendants cannot discover (or depose) the individual plaintiff class members until after the trial of the common issues. Accordingly, the defendants may be unfairly forced to consider settling before the trial of the common issues on the basis of what they can afford rather than what the litigation may be worth, if anything. These arguments were not accepted by the Ontario and British Columbia legislatures, although they may still be of some assistance to defendants in opposing certification of class actions in specific cases.

This chapter will review the Canadian class action experience to date, emphasizing the experience in Ontario, and comment on whether the experience supports the argument that we can expect a large number of frivolous and abusive class actions in the future, or the argument that the class action legislation in Canada will improve access to justice and reduce the burden on the public purse without unfairness to defendants.

Legislation in Canada

Quebec was the first province to enact legislation expressly permitting class actions. It permits a person to seek authorization from the Court to bring a class action if, among other things, the claims of the members raise identical, similar or related questions of law or fact, and the facts alleged seem to justify the conclusions sought. The order authorizing the class action (the "certification order") will describe the group, identify the principal issues to be dealt with and require that notice be given in some fashion to class members. A member can request to be excluded from the class ("opt out") so long as that is done before a date stipulated in the certification order, and a person who does so will not be bound by any judgment in the proceeding. Any final judgment in the proceeding will bind any member who did not request to be excluded. The legislation does not expressly restrict the group or class that can be certified to persons who reside in Quebec, or whose claims have a connection with Quebec.

The *Ontario Class Proceedings Act* came into force on January 1, 1993, after more than a decade of discussion beginning with the Ontario Law Reform Commission's Report on Class Actions issued in 1982. The basic framework of the Ontario Act is similar to the Quebec legislation, although the provisions are different in a number of significant respects. A member of an identifiable class of two or more persons may ask the Court to certify the proceeding as a class proceeding where, among other things, the claims of the class members raise common issues and a class proceeding would be the preferable procedure for the resolution of the common issues. The Court shall not refuse to certify the class action merely because the relief claimed includes a claim for damages that will require individual assessment after determination of the common issues. The certification order will describe the class and the common issues, and specify how and when a class member can exercise a right to opt out of the class. Notice of the certification of the class and of the right to opt out must be given to the class members, and those who exercise this right will not be bound by any judgment on the common issues. The judgment will, however, bind all members of the class who have not opted out. As in Quebec, there is no express restriction on the composition of the class related to a member's connection with Ontario. Unlike Quebec, however, the Ontario legislation permits certification of either a plaintiff or a defendant class.

British Columbia joined Ontario and Quebec by adopting class action legislation on August 1, 1995. The British Columbia legislation permits the Court to certify either a plaintiff or defendant class if, among other things, there is an identifiable class of two or more persons, common issues are raised and a class proceeding would be the preferable procedure for the fair and efficient resolution of the common issues. As in the Ontario legislation, there is no review of the merits of the proceeding on the certification motion except to confirm that the pleadings disclose a cause of action. The British Columbia Act restricts the persons who can be members of the class to residents of British Columbia or non-residents who opt into the class.

Both the Ontario and Quebec governments established funds that can, in appropriate cases, be used to defray legal expenses of a representative plaintiff. The Ontario fund is only to be used to defray disbursements (out-of-pocket expenses other than legal fees) whereas the Quebec fund can also be used to defray counsel fees.

When class action reform was proposed by the Ontario Law Reform Commission, it acknowledged that people would generally be reluctant to come forward and act as plaintiff representatives if they were liable to the normal "loser-pays" costs rule whereby an unsuccessful party in litigation in Ontario is obliged to pay a large portion of the successful party's legal expenses. The Commission recommended that, once a class action was certified, no party should be liable for costs except in the event of "vexatious, frivolous, or abusive conduct," but this proposal was not adopted when the Ontario Act was drafted. Instead both the Ontario and Quebec Acts provide that if a representative plaintiff receives funding from the government fund, he or she will no longer be exposed to the risk of having to pay the defendant's costs in the event the action is unsuccessful. In such cases, the defendant will be able to seek to recover its costs only from the government fund. British Columbia, on the other hand, adopted the Commission's approach of a "no costs" rule, whereby neither party is liable for the other's costs except where there has been frivolous, vexatious or abusive conduct.

Types of class actions that have been commenced

In the first twelve years of operation of the Quebec class action legislation, approximately 355 class actions were commenced in Quebec, for an average annual rate of approximately 30 cases.[1] Unlike Quebec, there is no central repository for information with respect to class actions started in Ontario, but it is estimated that there have been somewhere in the neighbourhood of 50 such proceedings commenced to date (or about 15 cases per year). Approximately 15 class actions have been commenced in British Columbia since its legislation was proclaimed in force one year ago.[2]

The following is a list of the types of proceedings that have been commenced as class proceedings in Ontario and British Columbia and, if known, an indication of whether or not the court certified the class action.[3]

Ontario

(1) Mass tort cases

- action on behalf of women who received silicone gel breast implants; approximately five such actions have been commenced in Ontario:—one was certified on a contested motion, one was certified on consent for settlement purposes, two have not proceeded to a certification motion, and one was dismissed on the basis that it was statute barred, although this is under appeal
- action commenced to recover damages for people who contracted HIV as a result of receiving contaminated blood and blood products:—certification refused
- action commenced by recipients of allegedly defective heart pacemaker leads:—certified
- action commenced on behalf of persons injured in a recent subway collision

- consumer action commenced by purchasers of household dryers who allege they were defective
- action commenced by homeowners alleged to have suffered damage to their homes as a result of the installation of defective plastic furnace venting systems
- action for damages allegedly suffered as a result of the release of toxic gases from a manufacturing facility
- consumer action related to the alleged use of lead based paint on miniblinds

(2) Contract/misrepresentation cases

- action by investors in a tax driven condominium development:—certification denied
- action commenced on behalf of equity members of a golf club against the developer of the project:—certified, but with substantial sub-classing of the plaintiffs' class
- action by credit card holders alleging improper calculation of interest charges:—dismissed on a summary judgment motion, before certification was sought
- consumer action alleging illegal calculation of interest rates by a utility; at least three such actions have been commenced:—one was dismissed on a motion for summary judgment prior to certification being sought
- application for an accounting with respect to oil well operations:—certified.
- action on behalf of ticket holders to a hockey game cancelled because of an National Hockey League strike:—dismissed before certification sought because the pleadings failed to disclose a cause of action and the claim was an abuse of process
- action by former shareholders who had sold shares based on alleged misrepresentations in an offering circular:—certified
- action by owners of condominiums against a developer for interest on monies paid as deposits:—certified (the defendant asserted a counterclaim also certified as a class action)

- action by purchasers of vinyl siding against installers, the mortgage finance company and the solicitors involved
- consumer action alleging false advertising
- action by students at a community college who had enrolled in a program that was subsequently cancelled by the provincial government
- action by investors against a trust company and the government regarding investments in syndicated mortgages
- action by service station owners against a franchise royalty company

(3) Miscellaneous

- claims for group defamation:—dismissed before a certification motion in two cases, not dismissed in another
- application seeking damages for oppression on behalf of all minority shareholders:—certification denied
- applications by an employer/pension plan administrator against a class of beneficiaries, to implement a settlement of a dispute as to entitlement to a pension plan surplus:—certified for settlement purposes
- action by pension beneficiaries to determine pension entitlements:—certified but summary judgment then granted dismissing the action
- action by members of a voluntary unincorporated association regarding an internal trade union dispute:—certified
- action by native band members claiming an interest in land:—certified (a defendants' class was also certified)
- application for a declaration that the Law Society and Ontario government were in breach of their statutory obligations to pay outstanding Legal Aid bills:—settled before certification sought
- action alleging negligence by the Law Society in failing to detect the misuse of lawyers' trust accounts
- action for failure to pay music royalties

- action to strike down the practice of deducting $100 from welfare cheques of immigrants whose sponsors defaulted, on the basis that the practice was discriminatory

British Columbia

(1) Mass tort cases

- action by women who received silicone gel breast implants:—certified
- action alleging defects in radiant ceiling heat panels:—certified
- action related to defective toilets:—certified.
- action commenced by recipients of allegedly defective heart pacemaker leads

(2) Miscellaneous

- bad faith action against the Insurance Corporation of British Columbia (ICBC) challenging its "minimal/no damage program" for handling auto accidents:—certification denied

As is apparent from the above, a number of cases have been disposed of on interlocutory motions prior to a certification application either because, on the pleadings, the claims did not state a reasonable cause of action, or because it was determined on a motion for summary judgment that the claim did not raise a genuine issue for trial.

Comparison of Canadian and American class action rules

The general structure of the legislation in the three Canadian provinces is similar to the American model. All provide for preliminary judicial certification of the class action, notice to the class members in some form, opting out by class members who wish to pursue their actions individually, trial of the common issues, possibility of aggregate assessment of damages, and subsequent proceedings to resolve individual issues.

There are, however, some significant differences. United States Federal Rule 23 governs class actions and permits them only if, among other things, the class is so numerous that joinder of the individual claims of the members is impracticable ("numerosity"), the common questions of law or fact predominate over any questions affecting only individual members and a class action is the superior method for the fair and efficient adjudication of the "controversy" (as opposed to just the common issues).

In the Ontario legislation, on the contrary, the test for certification does not include a "numerosity" requirement (*i.e.*, in Ontario, two class members would be sufficient) and the common issues do not need to predominate over the individual issues. The class action merely needs to be the preferable procedure for the resolution of the common issues themselves. Thus the Ontario legislation is drafted in a way that, in theory, can be expected to result in the certification of more class actions than would be certified in the United States.

There is a considerable inconsistency in the decisions of judges in Ontario on certification motions, so there is some difficulty in predicting when certification will be granted. In the only appellate decision on certification to date,[4] the Ontario Divisional Court confirmed that the common issues do not have to predominate over the individual ones. Nevertheless, the Court accepted that it could consider the individual issues involved in the litigation in determining whether a class proceeding would be the preferable procedure for the resolution of those issues that were common. The Court was particularly concerned that there were individual issues that would affect liability (such as reliance), and not just the assessment of damages. Some of the *obiter* comments made by at least one of the judges in the Divisional Court may result in a lower number of class actions being certified than expected from a review of the wording of the legislation. However, trial level decisions delivered since the Divisional Court's decision have not, by and large, adopted this more restrictive approach, and it appears that certification is still more likely to be granted in Ontario than in the United States. (There is a recent trend away from certifying mass tort claims in the United States, whereas in both Ontario and British Columbia, the courts have certified these types of actions notwithstanding that there may be a number of individual issues.)

With respect to certification, the wording of the British Columbia Act is somewhere between United States Federal Court Rule 23 and the Ontario provision. There is no "numerosity" requirement and the claims of the class members need only raise common issues "whether or not those common issues predominate over issues affecting only individual members." However, the Court is expressly permitted by the legislation, in determining whether a class proceeding would be the preferable procedure for the resolution of the common issues, to consider whether the common issues predominate over the individual issues. The British Columbia legislation essentially adopts the approach in the comments made by the Ontario Divisional Court.

In all three provinces, the Court's view as to whether a class action for the type of case in question will satisfy the objectives of the legislation—access to justice, reduced use of judicial resources and deterrence—will be a very significant factor in its decision on certification. In addition, it is the author's view that the Court's willingness to certify a class action has been and will continue to be, at least subconsciously, affected by its view of the merits of the proceeding, although under all of the legislation in Canada there is no requirement for the Court to review the merits. The legislation in each case states that the Court is merely to confirm that the pleadings disclose a cause of action or, in Quebec, that the facts alleged seem to justify the conclusions sought. (To the extent that the Quebec legislation requires any review of the merits, it is a minimal one.)

Economic disincentives to Canadian class actions

It has been persuasively argued, by Watson and McGowan in particular, that the economics of class actions will likely determine the volume of class actions that will be commenced.[5] As noted at the outset, one objection to class action suits is that, if the incentives are wrongly structured, the resulting economics can lead to a large number of often extortionate suits in which even blameless defendants may find it advisable to make some sort of payment. This has obviously not happened yet, and indeed there are a number of economic disincentives to class actions, at least under the Ontario Act, for both the representative plaintiff and plaintiff's counsel.

Disincentives to the representative plaintiff

A class representative who does not receive funding from the Class Proceedings Fund (and it is believed that few have in Ontario to date) is at risk of personal liability for the defendant's costs should the class action fail. Assuming that representative plaintiffs are properly advised of this risk, they ought to be reluctant to sue on behalf of a number of other people who do not take on any of that risk, unless the representative plaintiff has no assets against which a costs order could be executed. The representative plaintiff can only ever recover his or her own individual damages and will receive no premium or bonus for taking on the risk of an adverse costs award. The Ontario courts have dealt with the concern that the plaintiffs' class will chose a judgment-proof (that is, asset-free) plaintiff as the representative, by awarding costs against non-parties if, for example, the non-party promotes the action and purports to sell rights in the proceeds of the action to the public.

This economic disincentive is not present in British Columbia, which has a no-costs rule. A representative plaintiff will not be exposed to the risk of paying the defendant's legal costs if the action does not succeed, so long as that party is not guilty of vexatious, frivolous, or abusive conduct in the proceeding. It will be interesting to see if this difference results in more class actions there than in Ontario.

The Ontario Class Proceedings Fund is required to pay costs awarded to a successful defendant in cases where it provides funding. Given the Fund's limited capital base ($500,000.00), a single adverse costs award could deplete the entire Fund. Accordingly, the Fund can only afford to provide funding for Ontario cases with a very high prospect of success.

Disincentives to the plaintiff's counsel

Lawyers can be retained in Ontario to act for the plaintiff class on a contingent fee basis, which is not permitted for any other action that can be brought in Ontario. However, it was perceived by many, until the spring of 1996, that the Ontario Act did not allow lawyers to calculate their fees based on a percentage of the class recovery, but rather required a determination by the Court after the action had been resolved as to whether the lawyer was entitled to a "multiplier" on his or her normal fees (calculated based on the lawyer's hourly rate and the time spent on the matter) as compensation for the risk taken.

One incentive in the United States for plaintiffs' lawyers to undertake class actions is that the potential recovery by the lawyer can be enormous. In most cases the lawyer can request a percentage fee arrangement and, together with the prospect of a large jury award and a large punitive damage assessment, a plaintiff's lawyer could retire on one successful class action. This potential gain has resulted in American plaintiffs' counsel not only undertaking class actions but seeking them out through advertisement.

With the Ontario Act's costs provisions, it is not clear that there will be a sufficient potential gain for plaintiffs' lawyers to accept the risks involved in class action litigation. Plaintiffs' lawyers generally end up financing the litigation, both by paying disbursements with their own funds and by not billing for a lengthy period of time (often years) for the work that they do, wreaking havoc on the firm's cash flow.

However, last year, in the pacemaker leads litigation in Ontario, plaintiffs' counsel had the Court approve in advance a fixed fee per class member payable only in the event of success. The fixed fee arrangement was not based on a multiplier. The Ontario Act has since been held also to allow approved-in-advance percentage contingent fees.

Even if the Court of Appeal adopts the same interpretation of the Ontario Act, it will be some time before Ontario lawyers will likely be willing to take on the risks of these actions (in the absence of clear liability at least). Generally, law firms in Ontario are not set up to operate as a business under contingency fee arrangements and are not used to dealing with pure contingent fees. In personal injury work generally, plaintiffs' lawyers take on cases where they believe there is no real liability issue and where there will be some amount paid to the plaintiffs that can be used to pay lawyers' fees. The lawyer in these situations, however, recognizes that he or she will not be paid if the action is unsuccessful and, accordingly, will not be willing to take on a doubtful case. It is likely that plaintiffs' lawyers in Ontario will, at least in the near future, continue to assess class actions on the same basis, and will only be willing to take on the financial risks involved in such actions where they believe there is little doubt that the action will be successful. British Columbia has had contingency fees for some time and, accordingly, plaintiffs' counsel there may not have the same reluctance to getting involved in this type of litigation.

A decision of an Ontario General Division judge in July of last year may cause plaintiffs' lawyers in Ontario to be even more reluctant to take on these types of cases. The judge heard an application to fix a multiplier for the fees of the plaintiffs' lawyer in a successful securities class action related to the Maple Leaf Gardens litigation. The Court, with the benefit of hindsight, was of the view that the hours spent by the lawyers were excessive, that the hourly rates (which the representative plaintiff had agreed to and which, therefore, could not be challenged) were too high, and that there was little or no risk taken on by the lawyers. He accordingly approved a very low multiplier (1.5). The risk of judges adopting this approach to the fees of successful plaintiffs' counsel will be a further disincentive to their accepting the risks and financial burdens involved in class action litigation.

Finally, it should be noted that, both in Ontario and Quebec, plaintiffs' class counsel may be held personally liable for costs incurred without reasonable cause, although it is expected that this would be ordered in only the most unusual and extreme of cases.

Conclusion

The development of class actions in both Ontario and British Columbia is still in its infancy. The majority of cases decided to date are on issues related to when the actions will be approved by the court and to arrangements with plaintiffs' counsel regarding costs. Case law has not developed on a number of other significant points raised by the legislation and, even on the issues of certification and costs there are few appellate court decisions, leaving much uncertainty and, consequently, much risk in taking on this type of litigation both for the representative plaintiff and for plaintiffs' class counsel.

Despite these risks and the economic disincentives referred to above, there has been a modest number of class actions commenced in Ontario and British Columbia. Some of those actions would undoubtedly be described by defence counsel as frivolous and groundless, but there does not appear to have been an excessive amount of that sort of action. It can be expected that the use of class actions in Ontario, in the near future at least, will generally continue to be limited to those actions that are perceived by plaintiffs' counsel to have substantial merit and little likelihood of failure. The situation may be quite different in British Columbia because some of the economic disincentives have not been made part of its legislation.

A final note: it is not clear at present whether an action can be brought in one province in Canada on behalf of only the residents of that province or on behalf of similarly situated persons across the entire country regardless of their lack of connection with the forum province. Strong arguments can be made by defendants that such proceedings are unconstitutional and ought not to be permitted. However, trial level decisions of two Ontario judges and one British Columbia judge have approved "national class" proceedings.[6] If national class actions are permitted, as they are in the United States, there will be some ability for the plaintiff class to forum-shop and seek out the province perceived to have rules most advantageous to the plaintiff class. Accordingly, we will have to watch the developments of class actions in all three provinces closely to assess whether or not Canada is inheriting America's litigious legacy in this area. Up to this point, however, there simply is not enough material to render a verdict one way or the other on the likely ultimate impact of class actions on the quantity, quality, or fairness of litigation in Canada.

Notes

1 S. Potter and J-C Renée, Class Actions: Quebec's Experience in *Insight*, New Class Proceedings Legislation, April 11, 1991.

2 An article entitled Identify Prominent Issues Early in Class Actions, *Ontario Lawyers Weekly*, November 15, 1996, p. 13 identifies 9 commenced up to the date of the article and the total estimate of 15 is based on additional anecdotal evidence from lawyers in British Columbia.

3 For brevity and simplicity, the author has not included case references and citations. However, he would be pleased to do so on request and can be reached at Blake, Cassels & Graydon, Toronto, Ontario direct telephone number (416) 863-3884. See also Gary D. Watson, *A Stock Taking of Class Procedures in Ontario: Is the Price Wrong*, (Annual Workshop on Commercial and Consumer Law, University of Toronto Faculty of Law, October 21, 1995).

4 *Abdool* v. *Anaheim Management Ltd.* (1995), 21 O.R. (3d) 453 (Div. Ct.).

5 Watson and McGowan, Ontario's New Class Proceedings Legislation: An Analysis in the *Guide to Case Management and Class Proceedings* (supplement to Ontario Civil Practice 1995). See also the Ontario Law Reform Commission's *Report on Class Actions* (1982), p. 647.

6 *Nantais* v. *Telectronics Proprietary (Canada) Ltd.* (1995), 25 O.R. (3d) 331 (Gen. Div.); leave to appeal refused, at 347 (Gen. Div.); *Bendall* v. *McGhan Medical Corp.* (1993), 14 O.R. (3d) 734 (Gen. Div.); *Harrington* v. *Dow Corning Corp., et al.*, an unreported decision of Mr. Justice K.C. MacKenzie released February 14, 1997.

Dow Corning Breast Implant Action

RICHARD A. HAZLETON

If you have been living the silicone breast implant saga for most of this decade, it is easy to forget that those with whom you speak often are not aware of its details or even of the basic facts. Naturally some of my comments pertain to the particular circumstances prevailing at the time of writing, while others will be of more general application.

It is also important to keep in mind how different countries view this controversy and the device itself. In Japan, if one asked the man or woman in the street about the silicone breast implant controversy, they might respond by asking "what controversy?" In Australia, if one asked that same question, a fight might result, depending on who was asked. Canada seems to be somewhere in between.

Therefore it is important to start with some current information on breast implants and the status of Dow Corning. As many readers will be aware, we filed for bankruptcy under Chapter 11 of the United States Bankruptcy Code on May 15th of 1995. That decision was driven primarily by an avalanche of lawsuits that, despite our efforts, we were unable to resolve by any other means.

In the United States, the Chapter 11 process provides that when a firm, individual, or organization files for bankruptcy, all litigation against them is halted and they are given the opportunity to propose a plan of financial reorganisation that will satisfy any legitimate claims against them. Naturally, a bankruptcy court judge must approve the plan. Dow Corning is moving forward in that process and, while it is impossible to predict an exact date for completion, we are hopeful that we will emerge from Chapter 11 sometime in 1998. Meanwhile, fortunately, the rest of our business has been very strong.

Breast implants: the state of the art in successful unsound litigation

What makes this story interesting to those not directly involved in the litigation and its aftermath is that the breast implant controversy marks the current state of the art in how the plaintiffs' bar can drive a product from the market despite more than 30 years of largely safe and efficacious use. In 1991, there were 137 lawsuits against us for the product; three years later there were 19,000.

Over this period of time, the plaintiffs' bar launched an unprecedented attack against this medical device, conducting thousands of depositions, filing hundreds of motions against us and the other manufacturers, many of them passed electronically from attorney to attorney in such an assembly-line fashion that one finds the very same typographical errors in suits filed all across the country.

When this began, the silicone breast implant had been used by about a million women. During the more than 30 years that the device was on the market, we had conducted more than 300 studies of the device and its components. In addition, we had an equal number of years of human experience. As questions of non-life threatening complications arose—as they will with any device implanted into the human body—they were addressed and improvements were made.

What caused this controversy to explode, however, were allegations, based only on anecdotal reports fed into a near-hysterical media environment, that breast implants caused terrible autoimmune diseases in the women who used the product.

In 1991, Dow Corning had several large-scale epidemiology studies on those questions underway but the results were not in yet. During 1992 and 1993, scientists both in the United States and around the world began their own studies. Today, there are more than 20 research studies, performed by prestigious medical research institutions around the world including the University of Toronto in Canada, the Mayo Clinic, the Harvard Medical School, University of Michigan and the Johns Hopkins University. All of the studies showed no substantial increased risk of systemic disease among women with breast implants.

When I talk with my Canadian or European colleagues they always ask, how could this have happened? How could a successful, innovative company like Dow Corning, which has prided itself on its ethics, end up in bankruptcy because of one of 5,000 products the company manufactures?

Litigation, Incorporated

The primary reason, in our estimation, is what we call Litigation, Incorporated. And what we mean by that is that litigation, as it is now practised, has evolved from a process to provide justice in accordance with professional principles into a business predicated on economic incentives.

In my judgement, this is inherently undesirable, for the original intention of the civil justice system was to adjudicate fairly the alleged damages incurred by a plaintiff, and that is not its effect today. In the United States in 1997, Litigation, Incorporated is seeking the richest market offering the greatest returns in ways that distort one of the fundamental principles of this nation: fair and equitable justice.

It may be alleged that this is both natural and desirable, that everyone in business is trying, and should be trying, to make money, get ahead and provide for their families. And indeed they are, but there is a crucial difference between what most companies do and what Litigation, Incorporated does.

Dow Corning, like most corporations, is in business under a stable set of rules governing fair, voluntary exchange, to produce products that make our customers more productive and profitable and, directly or indirectly, improve the quality of life for consumers. When we succeed, our customers succeed, our suppliers succeed, our employees succeed, and economies around the world succeed.

When Litigation, Incorporated succeeds, almost the exact opposite occurs. Because it operates under rules that are not stable and that do not promote fair, voluntary exchange, its activities harm all but a tiny handful of people. Even among plaintiffs, justice is not done predictably and often is not done at all. Undoubtedly, some people who have been injured by a dangerous product or service are compensated. But this process operates more in the fashion of a lottery or on the basis of who can get to the head of the queue at the courthouse, rather than on the basis of who has the most valid claim. And it is not necessary. Canada and other nations have provided consumer protection without the problems we've created.

A system under which everyone loses

Increasingly, all Americans are losers under the current system. One of the most often debated topics in Washington is tort reform, but it never seems to resonate with consumers. It gets dismissed as simply a business issue, of little consequence to the average person or worse, as an issue of consumer victim versus evil, greedy corporations. Nothing could be further from the truth.

This is not about companies battling attorneys in court. This is about people losing access to important medical technology. All of us will collectively bear the costs of mammoth jury verdicts that are truly an American phenomenon through higher insurance premiums and increases in the costs of the goods and services we all buy.

When the end game of litigation becomes simply the largest economic prize—won largely by chance, like roulette, rather than by the orderly operation of a system that protects the rights of those who have been truly injured—we all lose. Innovation has no loyalty. It cannot flourish where entrepreneurs are punished rather than rewarded for their efforts. At best, it will move off shore. At worst, it will wither and die.

And there are more direct victims of this system. In the case of breast implants, countless women are terrified by what they have been led to believe about their implants and have become understandably desperate to find relief from their illnesses. In their desperation, they have been led into horrendously expensive diagnostic and treatment regimes by some medical practitioners who are the plaintiff's attorneys' strategic partners in Litigation, Incorporated. These schemes are merely useless for the most fortunate women, and health-threatening in their own right for others less fortunate.

Certainly breast implants cause local complications and can rupture. We intend to compensate legitimate claims on those issues as we resolve our Chapter 11 case just as we have in the past. However, as Dow Corning sits in Chapter 11 despite no valid scientific studies demonstrating that silicone breast implants cause systemic illness, I often wonder what it will take for the United States to wake up to the very real price we will all pay if our civil justice system is not reformed.

Lessons

What lessons can be drawn from our experience? First and most generally, try to keep the best of what you already have while avoiding the abuses that have distorted the American system. In practical terms, that means retaining a loser-pays rule and avoiding the spread of the contingency fee system. These issues, along with often unlimited ability to obtain punitive damage awards, are what fuel the incentives that created Litigation, Incorporated in the United States.

Second, Canada should continue its practice of having judges, not juries, hear civil cases. This is not to criticize juries. They usually do their level best to understand the scientific evidence and render a fair judgement. However, as Dow Corning's experience has shown, juries' understandable sympathy toward plaintiffs who are sick or injured can lead them to blame and seek relief from innocent parties who simply happen to be wealthy and convenient. This sympathy can have particularly improper effects when a jury is trying with little success to sort through complex scientific issues.

The principle of "a trial before your peers" is justifiably a hallowed tradition in American jurisprudence, arising from our English common-law heritage. It should not be cast aside lightly. Nonetheless, the reality is that the ability of jurors not trained in scientific disciplines to understand fully what is presented to them is problematic at best. This is not a commentary on their intelligence and certainly not on their integrity—it is, rather, a commentary on the highly technical nature of the evidence they are asked to consider.

This leads to a much larger point that is critical to litigation such as ours, the issue of scientific evidence in the courtroom. As Dr. Marcia Angell, editor of the *New England Journal of Medicine* says in her recent book, *Science on Trial*, whether or not silicone breast implants cause diseases is not a matter of opinion or of a scorecard of "yes" and "no" jury verdicts. It is a matter of biological fact for science to decide. Women who have been featured on several of the investigative television shows in the United States say that they don't need any evidence—*they are the evidence!*

They could, in fact, be part of the evidence, but their cases—like everyone else's—need to be evaluated in the context of thousands of women examined in epidemiology studies carefully designed to determine if the incidence of a disease is any greater among the population being studied than it is among a control population. The sad truth is that a small proportion of people have medical problems, severe or otherwise, whose origin simply cannot be determined. This naturally includes some women who have had breast implants. But unless the proportion of those with breast implants who also have otherwise inexplicable medical problems is higher than the proportion in the population at large, there is no indication that implants pose an increased health risk to women who have devices.

In the case of breast implants, there simply is no such causal link. There is no higher incidence of disease among women with breast implants. The plaintiffs' attorneys cannot offer one valid scientific study to prove their case. Instead, they rely on highly-paid, so-called medical experts—a part of Litigation, Incorporated—who offer theories of cause and effect that are shared by few others in the medical or scientific communities and are well-paid for doing so. This is an example of my contention that Litigation, Incorporated is not like a normal business because of the rules it operates under.

Fortunately, our judicial system—including the United States Supreme Court—is starting to recognize this problem and to alter the rules to enhance fairness and predictability. Three years ago that Court introduced the *Daubert* Principle as a result of the *Bendectin* morning-sickness-drug litigation. This principle instructs judges to become gatekeepers in their courtroom, allowing only testimony that enjoys widespread acceptance by the medical and scientific communities.

Some judges have gone further. Courts overseeing breast implant litigation have begun to appoint blue-ribbon panels of scientists to assist the judges in weighing the scientific evidence. The roles of these panels is to evaluate all of the scientific evidence presented by both sides and to determine to what extent the methodology and results represented by this evidence enjoy wide recognition by the medical community. We at Dow Corning are optimistic that the work of a similar panel can be utilized in our Chapter 11 process.

Appropriate use of such panels and their advice can prevent unsubstantiated junk-science theories from unduly influencing the outcome of litigation and return some level of sanity to the process of determining injury causation and liability. Such action is necessary, and as far as possible should be kept out of the political arena, another area where the operation of the rules is neither as predictable or as fair as it ought to be. When science takes a back seat to anecdote and emotion, it is very naïve to expect politicians to bail us out. Some politicians have even been known to use the breast implant controversy to their own advantage, while most are simply loath to take a position. They quite wisely recognize that they are in no position to make a scientific judgement, and quite cleverly realize that any responsible position they do take is likely to do them more political harm than good. The result, generally, is inactivity—or worse.

The best role, judicially as well as politically, that politicians can play is to encourage the regulatory agencies under their purview—who do have the requisite medical credentials—to follow the science wherever it goes, and to ensure that courts have the best possible opportunity to evaluate this science.

Health Canada, therefore, ought to be encouraged to take a more active role in the silicone breast implant controversy. Twenty-three studies have now been conducted basically giving the device a clean bill of health. The British Medical Devices Agency has performed an analysis of the world medical literature and has said there is no scientific basis for tying silicone breast implants to autoimmune illnesses. Despite this, Health Canada remains silent.

Given the American experience, it cannot be doubted that there are thousands of women with breast implants in Canada who would be greatly reassured if their government were simply to pass on to consumers—and endorse—the body of scientific evidence that has now been amassed. Health Canada has every assurance from Dow Corning that should the safety picture of breast implants change in any way, they will hear it from us. We are in the midst of a $30 million research program that is updating our existing research as we evaluate all of the silicones used in literally hundreds of thousands of products to ensure that we continue to know everything there is to know about them from a safety standpoint; this includes every component of breast implants. The only restriction we place on our outside researchers is that *whatever* their research results show, they must publish them.

In closing, I would urge this audience not to be complacent about the threat of runaway mass tort litigation of the sort that has driven Dow Corning into Chapter 11 bankruptcy proceedings without a shred of justification, placing the livelihood of its employees and the well-being of its customers in quite unjustified jeopardy. Another contributor to this volume describes the consequences to one Canadian company of unfortunately catching the eye of a branch of Litigation, Incorporated, in the form of the plaintiffs' bar in Mississippi. Being forewarned is being forearmed. Canadians must let their elected officials know of their concerns and their determination to keep the Canadian civil justice system squarely balanced on the concepts of independent scientific evidence and fact, rather than emotion and anecdote.

The crucial measures toward this end are retaining the "loser-pays" principle and avoiding American-style contingency fees, continuing to have judges rather than juries hear tort cases, retaining and strengthening rational rules of evidence particularly on scientific issues, and keeping the issue out of the political arena insofar as possible.

Some Economics of the Canadian Legal Profession

STEPHEN T. EASTON

The nature of the evidence

The usual analysis an economist would like to do with the legal profession is look at supply and demand. How many lawyers are there and how much are their services worth? What are the forces that change the number of lawyers, the extent of their practices, and the prices that they receive for the services that they render? In Canada at the present time, it is not really possible to do this. The data characterizing the legal profession are not sufficiently fine to support such a construction. Any analysis must of necessity be more limited. But even without a full description of the economic geography of supply and demand, past and current trends provide landmarks and lookout points of interest.

The single most striking characteristic of the Canadian legal profession from an outsider's perspective is the expansion of the number of participants in the industry. From 1985 to 1995, the

Notes will be found on page 86.

number of members of the Canadian Bar Association increased by 37 percent. During this same period the population of Canada grew only 13 percent.

The reasons for, and consequences of, this dramatic expansion need to be explained because they will guide the development of the legal environment in Canada for the next half-century. If it is the case that the complexity of society requires more and more legal advice to function, then we might think of the increase in the number of lawyers as being demand-driven and also socially beneficial. This would be associated with both higher numbers of lawyers and higher prices being paid for their services. It is also possible that individuals and organizations need more and more legal advice because of changes in the rules of litigation or the opening up of new areas for litigation that are not in fact socially beneficial. This too would be associated with both higher numbers of lawyers and higher prices for their services.

But there is another possibility: the increase in the legal population has been supply driven. If more lawyers have been entering the market over the past few years than is warranted even by the increasing amount of legal work, then we might anticipate that the average amount of money paid for a unit of legal services would decrease. This seems to be what is happening.

Traditional legal services have, for the most part, been a highly efficient aspect of smoothly functioning private markets based on voluntary contract, and thus their expansion as the economy grows would be both natural and desirable. This is not necessarily true of changes in the rules to permit more litigation per unit of economic production, especially if a motive force behind the changes is lawyers with idle hands and shrinking bank accounts looking for new sources of income.

My hypothesis throughout this chapter is that we are observing at least in part a supply-driven phenomenon. Further, even if this is not the case, there is likely to be a reduction in some of the traditional sources of the demand for legal services in the next few years, which suggests that the focus of legal activity will be changing. In particular, the emphasis on civil litigation will become more pronounced as lawyers explore additional ways of using their skills beyond those associated with the traditional criminal and civil law. In either case, we face the prospect of lawyers seeking to use or change the rules to allow them to create more business to make up for the fall in the price of their services. Pressures from within the legal profession itself may contribute to an increase in socially undesirable litigation. Much of what I have to say is speculative. But even with the limited data at hand, there is much to speculate about.

Figure 1 Lawyers per million population, 1951 to 1991

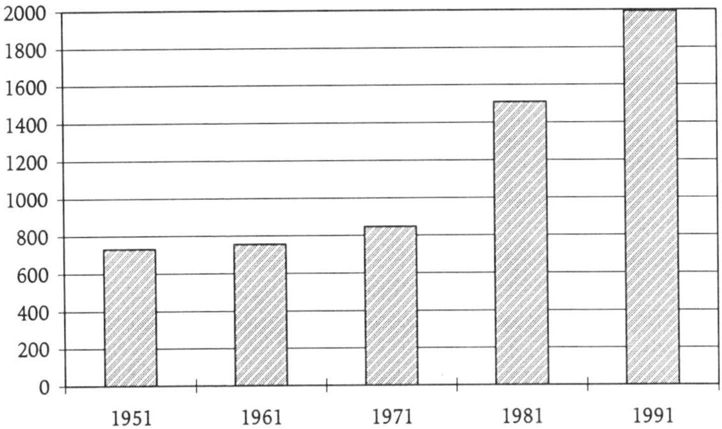

The number of lawyers

Since 1985, the number of lawyers in Canada has increased significantly. Figure 1 pieces together a visual description of the number of lawyers per million of population in Canada over the past 40 years, while figure 2 emphasizes the past decade. As is apparent there has been a steady increase in the number of lawyers both in the long and in the short run. This is faster than the overall growth in service sector output. As the fraction of services in the Canadian economy, services have increased from less than 50 percent of GDP in the early 1950s to over 66 percent in the today. From 1985, the increase in the share of output attributable to services has risen less rapidly—from 64 percent to 66 percent.

In the column headed "Membership," table 1 shows the increase in the absolute numbers of those listed by the Federation of Law Societies. This is a substantial increase over the past decade as the number of lawyers rose from 45,675 to 62,637. Looking at the growth in the numbers of lawyers per million of the general population provides another way to see the increase. This is displayed in the rightmost column as we grew from 1,750 per million in 1986 to over 2,100 in 1995.

Figure 2 Lawyers per million population, 1985 to 1995

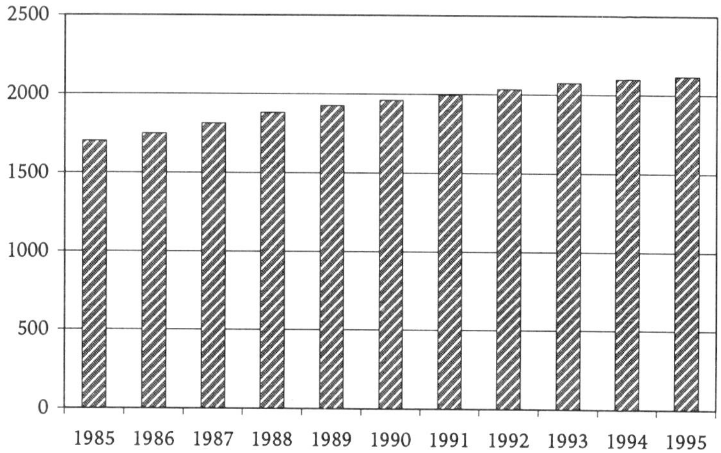

Lawyers and efficiency

It is not necessarily true, of course, that the sharp increase in the number of lawyers is undesirable. We live in a much more complex society today than in times past. Issues such as intellectual property rights will undoubtedly play an increasingly important role in the future. More lawyers will be needed for many reasons. But it is still the case that we have to feed many more legally credentialled mouths, and it is this issue to which we need to pay some attention. Some negative evidence does exist on this score. As a pure statistical matter, Brock, Magee, and Young (1985) find that the rate of economic growth of a country was lower as a function of the number of lawyers. In their analysis, they standardized for the level of economic development but they did not try to compare legal systems. Though far from conclusive, we should nonetheless be interested in the rapid increase in the numbers of lawyers being trained. What they are doing and why they are doing it is important. The focus of this book is upon the question whether or not the kinds of changes that may be taking place in the legal profession are desirable from different perspectives.

Canada is not the only common-law jurisdiction with many lawyers. In comparison to the United States in 1993, we have only about two-thirds as many lawyers per capita. However, it is also the case that we are training more, faster. In 1971, Canada had half as many lawyers as the United States; by 1981 the figure was 60 percent. Figure 3 points to the rapid increase in the proportion of lawyers in Canada relative to the United States. In the past few years (not shown in the figure), the per-capita number of lawyers in the United States has actually declined slightly, while the number in Canada continues to increase. As an absolute fraction of the population devoted to the legal profession, however, the United States continues to dominate. But the trend is at least loosely suggestive of a convergence between our system and theirs.

Figure 3 Canadian and American lawyers per million population, 1951 to 1991

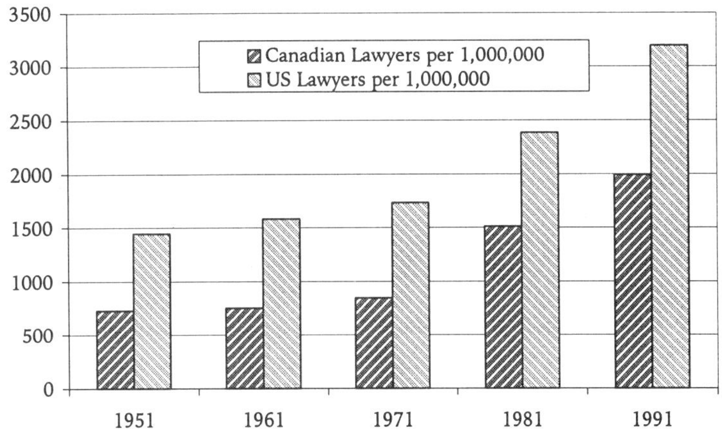

If Canada is to have an increasing number of lawyers in the future, there are a number of questions that come immediately to mind. Will the number of lawyers mirror the activities of those who have been in the profession in the past? Or will there likely be changes in the kinds of activities to which the new and larger numbers of professionals will need to turn to earn their keep?

Sources of traditional demand for legal services

Although it is certainly the case that the general public associates the legal system with crime and punishment, the crime rate cannot explain the pattern of persistent growth displayed in table 1.

In fact, since 1986 the crime rate rose until 1991 and has fallen back gradually since then. This is in contrast to the steady increase in the number of lawyers. Table 2 displays the number of criminal code incidents per 100,000 of population. It clearly has little to do with the increase in the number of lawyers.

Table 1 Membership in the Federation of Law Societies from 1986 to 1995

Year	Membership	Lawyers per 1,000,000 of Population
1986	45,675	1,748
1987	47,955	1,813
1988	50,397	1,882
1989	52,486	1,926
1990	54,256	1,961
1991	56,080	1,994
1992	58,019	2,033
1993	59,982	2,072
1994	61,317	2,096
1995	62,637	2,116

Further, we should expect the demographic structure of the Canadian population to continue to support a falling measured crime rate. Most of the people caught for crimes are males between the ages of 15 and 29. The fraction of the Canadian population in this range is forecast to be declining for the next quarter century from a current rate of 10.7 percent to a level of 9.7 percent.[1] Although many other factors than mere age are involved in the changing crime statistics, certainly the potential change in the demand for legal representation in criminal litigation in Canada will be different, were this segment of the population growing.

Legal aid as a source of income

One of the reliable sources of income for Canadian lawyers since the early 1980s has been the legal aid system. Legal aid expenditures have grown substantially since they were instituted in the early 1970s.[2] Although legal aid expenditures are not a large part of the income earned by all lawyers, it has been a very steady and growing component of income that is suddenly turning variable.[3] Since 1970/71, when legal aid constituted $12 million to a high water mark in 1993 at $670 million (1995 dollars), expenditures on legal aid—both criminal and civil—have expanded enormously.[4]

Table 2 The behaviour of the crime rate

Year	Criminal Code Incidents per 100,000
1986	8,984
1987	9,227
1988	9,234
1989	9,266
1990	9,904
1991	10,736
1992	10,394
1993	9,985
1994	9,684
1995	9,537

This source of income, however, is likely to take a significant reduction in the near term. In the largest provinces, Ontario, Quebec and British Columbia, the number of certificates issued for legal aid work has been, is, or is about to be diminished significantly.[5] For example in Ontario—the province that has spent almost half of the legal aid dollars in Canada—although the cost per case has been kept about the same in the past few years, the number of legal aid cases has gyrated as governments of all political stripes have tried to reconcile budgetary objectives (see table 3).

Reductions in caseload and overall costs are a concern to all provinces. Throughout Canada there is a worry that costs of legal aid have gotten out of hand and that some restrictions are appropriate and necessary.

It is interesting, however, to see the direction that the legal-aid caseload has taken. While in large part we think of legal aid as the legal system's aid in enforcing a fair argument for people who risk their liberty in criminal matters, over the past decade, more and more legal aid has been in the context of civil cases. In

Ontario, from over 60 percent of legal aid cases being criminal cases, in 1995 only 54 percent of cases were criminal cases. Although this trend is not national since legal aid is idiosyncratic by province, there is a tendency for civil legal aid costs per case to be rising faster than those in criminal matters. Thus relatively more resources have tended to be directed toward civil cases in the recent past although current budgetary redeployments and retrenchments may change this loose pattern.

Table 3 Legal aid caseload in Ontario from 1990 to1995

Year	Ontario Legal Aid Caseload
1990	108,033
1991	130,132
1992	160,221
1993	184,539
1994	148,406
1995	166,373

So where does this leave us? We have a legal system that faces reduced caseload from criminal work. There is both a reduction in the number of crimes being committed and a reduction in the number of legal aid cases. Resources devoted to civil justice issues have been increasing. This is the tableau against which the rapid expansion in the number of lawyers must be set.

Other sources of income

There are any number of other trends affecting lawyers' income. British Columbia is toying with no-fault auto insurance, a path already trodden in Ontario and other provinces. No-fault divorce is another source of reduced demand.

So where have the increases been in the sources of revenue for lawyers in the civil arena? Upon initiating research in the civil justice field, researchers at The Fraser Institute were astonished to find that there was little or no statistical information in Canada about the civil justice system, and remarkably little about the justice system at all (Lippert, Easton, and Yirush 1996).

For example, it is impossible to catalogue the number of civil justice cases taking place in Canada on an annual basis. Many jurisdictions do not keep appropriate records. Similarly, it is impossible to talk about efficiency in the courts in anything other than an extremely cavalier fashion. This is an increasingly important problem for courts and lawyers now that the justice system is called upon to take cuts as if it were any other part of the provincial budget. Yet there is no sense in which the courts are efficient; that is, that best practices for case management are used, that appropriate accounting is kept of expenditures of court time versus pre-court conferencing and so on. For example, there is no cost to leaving civil cases filed even when the parties have long since settled or abandoned an action. This clutters the books and can lead to very misleading estimates of caseload backlog.

The importance of record keeping (or its lack) by the judiciary or any statistical agency means that it is impossible to have a precise idea about the evolution of legal caseload. We do not have a systematic way of discriminating among cases. We do not have a good idea about the relative importance of liability cases versus contract cases. How many and how important are they? How quickly are class action cases increasing? In a survey of corporate counsel, The Fraser Institute in conjunction with the Canadian Bar Association and the Canadian Corporate Counsel Association attempted to get some kind of a picture of what has been taking place. But future surveys will be necessary to provide comparative data.

In the absence of quantitative information about caseload, we can get a sense of the importance of different sectors of the business to the legal profession by looking at spending and income of different parts of the legal system.

Column 1 in table 4 reports the average real growth in receipts by private law firms. Although there are many caveats with these numbers (Lippert, Easton, and Yirush 1996), except for the period of the mid-1980s the growth in receipts by law firms has not been very substantial. In contrast to the growth in spending on court and regulatory agencies, the legal profession has lagged in two of the three periods we examined. These figures have been adjusted to take account of inflation—hence the term "real."

What is apparent from the figures on income is that there has been little increase during the period of the rapid run-up of the number of lawyers. It suggests that the increase in the number of lawyers has not been matched by an increase in the kind of case law that has been traditionally been done by lawyers. It is both natural and understandable that the kinds of law that lawyers will pursue in the future will be different than the kind of law practised in the past. The market will need to be expanded. The traditional sources of demand have not increased to keep up with the supply and we foresee little by way of increases in the future among the types of demand—criminal, legal aid, and even some kinds of injury claims. It is this kind of expansion that we need to investigate to make sure that it is not damaging rather than useful. Such an expansion may be socially beneficial if the present system fails to safeguard rights efficiently and changes are made that do enhance efficiency. It will not help the economy to be efficient if the changes that are made are driven by the need of lawyers for more work.

Table 4 Average annual real growth of civil legal receipts by major recipient groups from 1973/74 to 1993/94

Years	Growth of Receipts of Private Law Firms	Growth of Court and Justice Personnel and Other Costs*	Growth of Regulatory Agencies and Tribunals Salaries and Costs
1974–1980	0.00%	7.20%	4.70%
1980–1987	6.30%	5.60%	1.20%
1987–1994	-0.30%	2.40%	1.30%

Source: Lippert, Easton, and Yirush 1996.

* These costs include salaries and benefits, court services, transportation and a pro-rata share of other fixed costs drawn from the public accounts.

Consequences for the legal environment

In any case, changes in the law should be weighed carefully against the danger, discussed by the Chief Justice and Attorney General of Ontario elsewhere in this book and testified to by many participants, that the volume of cases is already overwhelming the machinery of both civil and criminal justice in Canada. The gradual breakdown of the civil justice environment has already begun to take place if we listen to the participant. There have already been court-ordered releases of potential felons because delays were too long in the criminal courts. Many have complained about the delays that are clogging the civil system in particular courts.

In trying to get an sense of the magnitude of the problems facing the Canadian civil justice system, The Fraser Institute, together with the Canadian Bar Association and the Canadian Corporate Counsel Association, surveyed a sample of Corporate Counsel about the kinds of problems that they were facing with respect to their caseload. In our sample, corporate counsel dealt with an average of 58 cases each year during the last five years. Most (38 percent) of these cases were about contract law, while 14 percent involved labour or employment issues. Personal injury, product law, and tax matters were the subject of, respectively, 11, 8, and 5 percent of reported cases. Parties to the case were other companies in 46 percent of all cases and individuals in 41 percent of cases. Governments and government agencies at all levels were evenly split and totaled 10 percent of cases. Unions were involved in about 3 percent of cases.

The average counsel who completed the questionnaire began work on the case 10 months after the dispute began. The final disposition took 39 months on average although, if the case went to trial, it took 47 months. Comments by counsel included: "trials: take too long; [and are] too costly;" and "[t]he plaintiff in this case did nothing to move it forward for, literally, years and there was nothing in the court procedures to prevent that."

While such observations are certainly not definitive, they suggest that there are already difficulties that are associated with clogged resources. With the potential expansion of the kinds of civil justice issues that will be explored in other chapters of this in the areas of liability, class actions, tribunal appeals, and the like, it would be a miracle if the system is not seriously slowed in the next decade or two.

Conclusion

The thesis of this paper is that the legal profession is expanding in numbers even faster than it is expanding in revenue, that it is likely to continue to do so, and that this creates the danger of supply-driven and socially harmful increases in litigation. Traditional sources of income such as legal aid are likely to contract in the near future, and provinces are considering a number of strategies that are (potentially) income-reducing for the legal profession.

What kinds of questions arise from the analysis developed above? In terms of the legal profession, it seems to be clear that there will be a gradual change in the kinds of law that is being practised. What kind of law is valued in practice and what is being taught in the law schools today? We need to get a fix on the kind of new law that is being proposed. For example, what kind of restrictions should there be on class actions? Are lawyers receiving the kind of training that is appropriate to the current legal environment? Do we as a society want to encourage the expansion of law in one direction or another? It would seem reasonable that with the continuing development of the service industries and the consequent new emphasis on intellectual property whether disseminated over the Internet or through traditional channels, more and new law will be made. Yet the increase in the number of lawyers is probably in part not associated with these trends. How we assess the costs to the economy of expanded legal activity in nuisance suits and speculative liability challenges is probably an area that Canadians had better be prepared to investigate. There are too many new lawyers to split the traditional pie. Sending them into the kitchen to bake a new pie, however, may leave the rest of us with less for our own meals.

Notes

1 World Bank population forecast.
2 See for example Easton, Brantingham and Brantingham 1994.
3 Probably in the order of magnitude of 10 percent of all spending on legal services.
4 Even adjusted for inflation, the 1970 number of $12 million is no more than $40 million in today's dollars.
5 In June of 1996, Quebec amended the Legal Aid Act although caseload had remained more or less the same since 1991/92.

References

Easton, Stephen T., Paul J. Brantingham, and Patricia L. Brantingham (1994). *Legal Aid: Efficiency, Cost and Competitiveness*. Government and Competitiveness: School of Policy Studies, Queen's University.

Lippert, Owen, Stephen T. Easton, and Craig Yirush (1996). Trends in Canadian Civil Justice (revised) The original was presented to the Canadian Bar Association's Task Force on Civil Justice, February.

Magee, Stephen P., William A. Brock, and Leslie Young (1989). *Black Hole Tariffs and Endogenous Policy Theory.* Cambridge University Press.

World Bank data on diskette. *World Tables, 1995.*

Civil Liability in Canada
No Tip, No Iceberg

BRUCE FELDTHUSEN

It would be ambitious, if not presumptuous, to attempt in one short chapter to isolate all Canadian tort liability rules with a significant market impact. The focus here, following a few comments about general trends, will be on a number of specific topics most of which have proven controversial in the United States. Even so, readers must be forgiving if the analysis is not quite as exhaustive as they might have liked. It appears, based on this review of the situation, that the threat of an American-style litigation explosion in Canada is not very serious.

Most of the issues discussed in this chapter fall under provincial jurisdiction in Canada, and concern almost exclusively judge-made common law. Tort law is judge-made common law everywhere in Canada, except in Quebec where it is codified in the Civil Code of Quebec.[1] With the exception of the various statutory no-fault automobile insurance plans, there have been virtually no major Canadian legislative interventions. Nor, in contrast to the American situation, has there yet been much pressure for legislative tort reform. This probably reflects both a

Notes will be found on pages 102–105.

lesser need for reform, and weaker interest group lobbying by consumer, professional, and bar associations.

The Americanization of Canadian law

It will become apparent that there exist both similarities and significant differences between United States and Canadian tort law. Doctrine aside, there are also substantial differences between the legal cultures of the two countries that are reflected in the civil justice systems. For example, in the United States there is more civil litigation, more cases are decided by juries, and compensatory damage awards tend to be much higher. These differences should be carefully noted but, more importantly, not too much should be made of them.

Increasingly, and soon, tort law in Canada will come to resemble more closely tort law in the United States for two reasons. First, tort reform in the United States is inevitable, and some reforms may move United States doctrine toward the more conservative Canadian rules. Second, the Americanization of Canadian doctrine is also inevitable. We have seen it in all our corporate and commercial legislation. We have borrowed heavily from American experience in drafting and interpreting our Charter of Rights and Freedoms. Electronic access to American legal materials is already as good or better than electronic access to Canadian sources. United States tort precedents now appear frequently and prominently in Canadian appellate court opinions. Given the geographical and commercial similarities between the countries, some sort of convergence is both understandable and desirable. It is, of course, a different question as to precisely where we should converge.

The growth of negligence law: *prima facie* duty of care

The number and types of situations that may culminate in tort liability in Canada has increased dramatically this century, particularly over the past thirty years. Most innovation in Canadian tort law has occurred in negligence, specifically through the recognition of new duties of care.[2] Formally speaking, whether the defendant owes a duty of care to the plaintiff is a question of law for the judge alone. Careless conduct in the absence of a recognized duty of care is not actionable. The judge decides whether the facts pleaded support a legitimate legal claim. The judge is the legal gatekeeper.

It is axiomatic that a duty of care exists with respect to any allegation of foreseeable direct injury to person or property. Until approximately twenty years ago, if the defendant's alleged wrongdoing fell outside that paradigm, the law would recognize only special limited duties of care, if any duty at all. For example, the duties governing claims based on the defendant's negligent failure to act for the plaintiff's benefit, or claims for pure financial loss, were few and narrowly defined. This is no longer true.

The British House of Lords, which functions as Britain's Supreme Court, made a decision in *Anns* v. *London Borough of Merton* that signified an important new approach. British precedent is not binding on Canadian courts the way decisions by our own Supreme Court are, but because of the similarity in our legal traditions it can be extremely influential. In *Anns*, the House of Lords adopted a two-stage test for recognition of a duty of care. The first stage was decidedly pro-plaintiff. It recognized a *prima facie* duty based on simple proximity or foreseeable harm to a foreseeable plaintiff. At the second stage, the defendant had the onus of establishing a reason why a duty should be negatived or limited.[3] Since then, many restrictive precedents have been overruled, and many new duties of care recognized. Defendants rarely succeed under branch two of the *Anns* test. In fact, courts rarely refer to it at all.[4]

Ironically, there was eventually a backlash against this pro-plaintiff trend in England even as it was spreading to Canada. In *Murphy* v. *Brentwood District Council*, the House of Lords overruled itself, and put *Anns* aside in favour of the restrictive approach to negligence law that had traditionally prevailed.[5] The immediate consequence of *Murphy* was effectively to immunize municipal governments from liability for failing to have discovered construction defects in premises the municipality was empowered to inspect. More restrictive rules soon emerged in other areas outside the physical damage paradigm. For example, it is now much more difficult to recover for nervous shock or pure economic loss in England than in Canada. This is tort reform English style.

As judicial conservatism began to dominate in the House of Lords, judicial nationalism seemed to take hold in the Supreme Court of Canada. Again and again, the Supreme Court expressed its preference for *Anns* over *Murphy* as the Canadian law of duty of care. It became difficult to imagine how any Canadian defendant could have a negligence claim dismissed on a preliminary motion,[6] provided the plaintiff had been prudent enough to utter the magic word "proximity" in the pleadings.[7] This is not the first time in Canadian history that an attempt to differentiate ourselves from the English has made us more like the Americans.

Legal liability is probably the most cumbersome, time-consuming, expensive mechanism a modern state could design to shift losses from one party to another. In automobile accident cases, for example, the transaction costs associated with litigation are so high that it is estimated that less than one half of every dollar spent on liability insurance ever gets to the successful plaintiff. In contrast, with no-fault worker's compensation schemes it is estimated that approximately 90 cents of ever funding dollar gets to a claimant. Accordingly, one would have thought that there would be a presumption against liability unless a compelling case for liability were made. The first stage in *Anns* does exactly the opposite, establishing a presumption of legal obligation whenever the defendant's act or omission creates a foreseeable risk of any sort to a foreseeable plaintiff. Such "double foreseeability" alone offers no meaningful justification for recognizing legal liability. Nor does it assume any more explanatory power if duty is justified on the basis of the vacuous term "proximity" as courts that follow *Anns* often tend to do. The first stage in *Anns* is no threshold at all. Virtually anything can meet the elastic concept of foreseeability. One rarely finds a Canadian court considering limiting or denying a duty of care anymore, let alone actually doing so.[8]

One of the consequences of this is that Canadian judges rarely perform a legal gatekeeper function in negligence anymore. Virtually any coherent allegation of actionable negligence can now proceed to the trier of fact for resolution. More negligence suits get filed than would otherwise, and a wider range of negligence duties emerges. Whether this is a good or bad thing in efficiency terms depends on a more specific analysis of the new duties than is possible here. There are, however, a few consequences for a rationally based market economy.

Legal rules, however rationally crafted, assume relatively less importance in a tort system that abandons the responsibility to define legal duty. The human quirks and biases of lawyers, judges, and jurors become more important. The definition of legal fault is not determined by social science, moral philosophy, or otherwise, by an intellectual judicial elite. Rather it emerges on an *ad hoc* basis, from case to case. Certainty in the law, always suspect, decreases further. Outcome prediction is better based on behavioural sciences than on doctrinal legal training. One suspects that concern for impecunious injury victims frequently supersedes the application of rational accident deterrence in the application of the standard of reasonable care.

Just how serious is this? Let us keep a sense of perspective. I once estimated that Canadian negligence law may actually address as few as 0.05 percent of all serious disability claims in the country. Tort law deals primarily with accidental injury.[9] Canadian tort law lags behind American law in making doctrinal and procedural changes that allow it to address effectively illness caused, for example, by dangerous products such as tobacco,[10] industrial and agricultural chemicals,[11] pharmaceuticals,[12] and so on. Only 10 percent of serious disability is caused by the types of accidents—automobile accidents, sports accidents, household slips and falls, for example—with which the Canadian tort system typically deals. Of that 10 percent, approximately half is dealt with on a no-fault basis through workers compensation or no-fault automobile insurance plans. Most of the remaining accidents are regarded by the victim as unavoidable or as the victim's own fault. The victims rarely consult a lawyer, let alone sue. Whether we follow *Anns* or *Murphy* suddenly seems insignificant.

In the commercial sphere, one cannot make the same educated guess about the market impact. New duties in misrepresentation[13] and products liability[14] have greatly expanded recovery for pure economic loss. Some of this results in entirely new liability. However, many of the new cases simply shift liability from where it had previously been allocated by contract to another party in the commercial chain. This seems, *prima facie,* wasteful. There is also considerable uncertainty about the scope of liability for relational economic loss that is also unnecessarily wasteful.[15]

Products liability

The most important change ever to affect product liability law in Canada will be the emergence of class action claims in three provinces, and eventually, one supposes, elsewhere.[16] This subject is given full treatment by S. Gordon McKee elsewhere in this volume. The main doctrinal difference relevant to the current discussion is that Canada never adopted the doctrine of strict liability for defective products that exists across the United States in various forms. Strict liability in American law is outlined in S402A(1) Restatement of Torts, Second as follows:

(1) One who sells any product in a defective condition unreasonably dangerous to the user or consumer or to his property is subject to liability for physical harm thereby caused to the ultimate user or consumer, or to his property, if

  (a) the seller is engaged in the business of selling such a product, and

  (b) it is expected to and does reach the user or consumer without substantial change in the condition in which it is sold.

In contrast, products liability in Canada is governed by basic negligence law in tort. That means that in addition to proving what the Restatement requires, the Canadian plaintiff must also prove that the defect in the product came about by negligence on the part of the defendant. The Canadian law is fault-based, whereas the United States law is "strict" liability for defect; that is, American manufacturers are responsible for preventing defects, not simply for taking all reasonable steps to prevent them.

In theory, if the two regimes were accurate and free of transaction costs, they would provide precisely the same safety incentives to the manufacturer. A defendant will always prevent an accident if prevention costs are lower than liability costs, and allow it if the reverse is true. This is so in negligence or strict liability. What differs is who pays for the so-called "unavoidable" accidents; that is, accidents that are cheaper to experience than to prevent.[17] With strict liability, the manufacturer pays; with negligence, the victim pays because it is not negligent for the manufacturer to refuse to spend more on prevention than the projected accident cost.

In practice, strict liability might be superior. Arguably, manufacturer negligence is difficult to prove. The full social losses experienced by all victims and those who depend upon them may be under-compensated in a negligence regime. Strict liability may be, in effect, a duplicitous way of bringing a more accurate estimate of the cost of avoidable accidents home to manufacturers. Transaction costs are lower when a major element in the case, negligence, is eliminated. Strict liability also does a better job of internalizing the cost of product-defect accidents by having sellers incorporate anticipated accident costs into price. Consumers are poorly positioned to estimate these costs when purchasing.

One must also consider whether the difference between the two standards actually affects the outcome of litigation as much as it might first appear. Keep in mind that statutory sales law, substantially similar in Canada and the United States, lies in the background to provide relief against the immediate seller. In negligence, we employ a doctrine in Canadian law called *res ipsa loquitur* (the thing speaks for itself) that permits the jury to infer negligence from the accident itself, which in practice brings us close to strict liability. There are few cases in Canadian law reports where the plaintiff has succeeded on all the elements of the action including proof of defect, but lost on the issue of negligence.

Although it may be more difficult to succeed in a products liability suit in Canada than in the United States, this has little to do with negligence *versus* strict liability or any other doctrinal difference. There have been a number of high profile cases in which Canadian plaintiffs have failed to prove the defendant's product was defective, although courts in the United States have held otherwise. For example, in *Stiles* v. *Beckett*[18] a British Columbia Supreme Court trial judge dismissed an action against Honda because the plaintiff had failed to prove the all-terrain vehicle (ATV) was defective. Many decisions in the United States had held the opposite. In another, *Privest Properties Ltd.* v. *W.R. Grace & Co. of Canada Ltd.*,[19] a British Columbia Supreme Court judge dismissed the first asbestos property damage case tried in Canada. The court held that the plaintiffs had failed to prove that a fire retardant spray was a health hazard to building occupants. In so doing, the judge disagreed explicitly with approximately one dozen successful suits against the American parent company in the United States.[20] Perhaps the real distinction was that the Canadian actions were tried by a judge without a jury.

Whatever its other merits or drawbacks, strict liability serves as a mandatory insurance scheme for unavoidable product-defect accidents, and this is a strange category of injury to be singled out for a separate insurance regime. Liability regimes, whether predicated on fault or not, are notoriously expensive compared to first party schemes. Strict liability is not an efficient insurance scheme for unavoidable product defect accidents compared to many other options. However, if the state wants to have a mandatory insurance scheme for unavoidable product defect accidents, and is unwilling to provide state-sponsored cover, or to require by law that victims obtain their own private cover, then it has no option but to implement strict liability.

Another issue that deserves attention is the manufacturer's duty to warn of dangers related to the use and misuse of the product. Canadian courts recently have held that a manufacturer does not have a duty to warn the consumer of known or obvious dangers. In the Ontario case, the Court of Appeal employed this principle to overturn a jury verdict of liability.[21] The Ontario Court relied on decisions from the United States in support of its holding, whereas a similar decision in British Columbia was proclaimed as a departure from American law.[22] It would appear again that doctrinal differences do not amount to much, but that judges may have more control than juries in Canada.

Also on the subject of duty to warn, reference should be made to the Supreme Court of Canada's decision in *Hollis* v. *Dow Corning Corp.*[23] For one thing, the court was very demanding about what warnings were required with a personal health product such as breast implants. For another, the court held that the manufacturer's failure to warn the patient's doctor would culminate in liability even if there was evidence that the doctor would not have passed the warning on to the patient had it been given. The plaintiff's lawyer thought the decision would have major repercussions in the health product area, at least.

> The court's holding that Dow's risk warnings were inadequate, its restriction of the "learned intermediary" defence, and its refusal to impose strict causation requirements on plaintiffs, could help the cases of tens of thousands of women who are involved in silicone breast implant class actions in Canada, Mr. McKinlay [the plaintiff's lawyer] predicted. He added that the principles adopted on the duty to warn and causation issues in the case apply to medical products liability cases—such as the HIV-tainted blood cases—as well as to other types of products liability cases. [24]

Malpractice

There seems to be a good deal less malpractice litigation in Canada, and malpractice insurance premiums are lower than in the United States. Once again, the explanation probably lies elsewhere than in doctrine. Professional malpractice law in Canada is basic negligence law. The professional is held to the standard of competence of the reasonable practitioner in a similar reference group; the reasonable sole practitioner, the reasonable heart surgeon, and so on.

Medical malpractice law is interesting, although not necessarily typical.[25] There have been some noteworthy decisions in the Supreme Court of Canada. In *Reibl* v. *Hughes*[26] the Court adopted the American concept of informed consent. In *Snell* v. *Farrell*,[27] many thought the court had relaxed somewhat the strict burden of causation, otherwise an often fatal hurdle in a malpractice claim. In *Norberg* v. *Wynrib*,[28] a physician was held liable for trading a patient drugs for sexual favours. The decision seemed to redefine the defence of consent by vitiating apparent consent obtained in a "power dependent" relationship. It also suggested the possibility of proceeding against doctors for breach of fiduciary duty, a more open-ended, pro-plaintiff action than negligence. With each decision, concerns were expressed that the floodgates of malpractice litigation had been opened. This has not happened.

One reason is that it remains expensive and uncertain to mount such a claim. One lawyer suggests that disbursements in the range of $100,000 are not unusual. It has been estimated that 80 percent of all claims fail. One of the main reasons why this is so is the Canadian Medical Protective Association, an organization that, among other things, co-ordinates all legal work on behalf of the profession.[29] Its members claim that it litigates to uphold the principles of the profession. Others wonder if the principle is to eliminate malpractice suits as a viable option for patients. Regardless, the results are impressive.

The real problem with medical malpractice litigation—and perhaps with other malpractice litigation—is the transaction cost: the expense of the process overshadows any possible efficiency gains from the outcome. Rightly or wrongly, from a fault perspective, it delivers little compensation to most who suffer losses at the hands of the profession. For this reason, supplementary no-fault insurance has been suggested for medical injury.[30]

The other professions that ought particularly to be mentioned are the auditors, accountants, and related financial professions. Liability for negligent professional financial advice is well-established in Canadian law,[31] and generally the rules for negligent misrepresentation are substantially similar in Canada and the United States.[32] The potential for ruinous liability exists, given the enormous losses that may follow from the slightest of negligence. One doctrinal concern is whether the adviser's exposure should be limited to losses suffered in the very transaction for which the advice was offered, or should be broader.[33] There exists considerable divergence of opinion in Canada and in the United States as to which option would be more efficient.[34]

Another concern is whether it is appropriate to hold auditors jointly and severally liable with other defendants, some of whom may be guilty of fraud that the auditor negligently failed to detect.[35] Joint and several liability means that once two or more co-defendants are found liable, the plaintiff may recover the full damages awarded from any of them. Each co-defendant is liable to make good the full loss to the successful plaintiff, notwithstanding how the responsibility may be apportioned among the defendants. It assumes tremendous practical significance when only one of the several defendants is solvent or insured. For example, a municipality may be held only 10 percent liable in comparison to the primary tortfeasor but, nevertheless, end up paying 100 percent of the damages, if the primary tortfeasor is bankrupt or otherwise unavailable to pay its share. This doctrine is under attack in several Canadian contexts, including municipal liability to which I now turn.

Municipal liability

Public authorities, including municipal governments, are immune from negligence liability when they exercise statutory discretion to make policy decisions.[36] They are not immune for operational negligence in implementing these policy decisions. The dividing line between policy and operational is broad and ambiguous, however, and it is generally agreed that the Supreme Court of Canada recognizes less immunity than courts elsewhere in the Commonwealth.[37] Municipal governments seem to be sued more frequently than other public authorities. Other than limited immunity, there are no unique liability rules for municipal governments. But there are some applications of standard rules that have caused concern.

First, Canada, unlike England but like many American states, holds builders and manufacturers liable for dangerous defects in buildings and products, whether or not the defect manifests itself in an accident.[38] Controversial in its own right,[39] liability for dangerous defects has proven especially onerous for municipalities. They are frequently held liable for failing to have detected defective construction when exercising their statutory powers of inspection. Typically, the builder is insolvent, in which case by virtue of joint and several liability,[40] municipalities become liable for the full cost of repair or reconstruction. The situation here is analogous to that with respect to products liability described above. If mandatory insolvent builder insurance is deemed necessary, there are more efficient ways of providing it than by municipal liability,[41] especially if standard deterrence theory is suspect in the public sector.

Joint and several liability is always a concern for any well-funded defendant. Municipalities often find themselves jointly and severally liable in situations other than those involving defective construction. Occupier's liability is the branch of tort law that governs the responsibility of those who occupy land toward other persons who come on to the land. Joint and several occupier's liability is a major concern for municipalities with large land holdings, especially park and recreation lands. A plaintiff who is able to have even the slightest liability apportioned to a municipality may be able to collect the entire judgement from the municipality.

Another area of concern is illustrated by the Supreme Court of Canada's decision in *Tock* v. *St. John Metropolitan Area Board*.[42] The court held that the municipality was liable in nuisance to a homeowner whose basement was flooded when a sewer backed up. The municipality was not negligent, but liability in nuisance is not predicated on fault. The court held, based on the permissive legislation authorizing municipal sewer construction (a common form of legislation), that the municipality was to be judged on exactly the same principles that would apply to private parties. Given that few private citizens voluntarily construct city-wide sewage systems, the analogy seems somewhat flawed.

In these days of financial crises in municipal budgets, liability costs are onerous. Lobbying to increase immunity, to limit joint and several liability, and to address the *Tock* exposure is underway. Legislative responses are rumoured to be in preparation, and indeed in some form they are inevitable.

Punitive damages

Punitive damages have not historically been significant in Canada. Prior to 1988, the largest reported punitive damage award in Canada was $50,000; most punitive awards were much smaller and, moreover, punitive damages were rarely awarded at all.[43] Between 1985 and 1995, however, there were more than 150 reported punitive damage awards, at least 16 of which were in excess of $50,000.[44] These 16 include an award of approximately $4,800,000 as an accounting for wrongful profits,[45] $1,000,000 as punishment for breach of an insurer's duty of good faith,[46] and $800,000 in a defamation action discussed below.[47] Punitive damage awards are also routine in sexual battery suits, one of the fastest growing areas of liability in the country, and are sometimes awarded when the sexual battery defendant has been punished already in the criminal courts.[48] The largest punitive award was $15,000,000 in an infringement of patent action when the defendant continued to market the product in issue after a preliminary injunction prohibiting same had been issued.[49] The size of the award was determined with reference to the considerable wealth of the corporate defendant. The defendant's wealth is a recognized consideration for punitive damages in Canadian law, although it has never been emphasized quite so clearly before.[50] The award was overturned on appeal, but not because of any concern about the amount of the award.[51]

Punitive damages are available in any tort action involving advertent wrongdoing where the defendant's conduct may be described as: "harsh, vindictive, reprehensible, and malicious."[52] This is not dissimilar to the threshold employed in most American states. There are two differences, however, that make Canadian punitive awards smaller and less common. First, the plaintiff must be the victim of the conduct deserving of punishment. For example, if one wished to punish a fast-food chain for marketing dangerously hot coffee, punitive damages would have to be quantified on a case-by-case basis, proportioned to the wrong done to each individual plaintiff; not awarded all in one suit in an amount large enough to punish the entire practice.[53] Class actions may have a major impact on the application of this rule. Second, the rationale is punishment, not deterrence. For example, I know of no Canadian decision to take the probability of the defendant's escaping detection of future wrongdoing into account when quantifying the punitive award, which does happen in the United States.

Although punitive awards are becoming more common and larger in Canada, I do not foresee anything approaching a crisis. On the contrary, they may well enhance efficiency considerably through effective deterrence of systematic wrongdoing, if courts were to begin to embrace a deterrence rationale. Also, more thought should be given to the advantages of selective quasi-privatization of criminal law through the use of punitive damages in areas where criminal law has proven ineffective. Sexual battery may be just such an area.

Defamation

The law of defamation is well beyond my area of expertise. However, it should be mentioned because it is the one obvious area in which Canadian law is more pro-plaintiff than the law in the United States. The Supreme Court of Canada recently upheld a jury verdict in defamation for $300,000 general damages, $500,000 aggravated damages, and $800,000 punitive damages to a plaintiff defamed in his capacity as a Crown Attorney.[54] Sounding very much like a court in the United States, the Supreme Court praised the unique abilities of a jury to quantify these damages, and expressed a strong reluctance to interfere. It held that the cap on general damages applied in personal injury cases did not apply in defamation.[55] It also declined expressly to adopt the reasoning of the United States Supreme Court in *New York Times Co.* v. *Sullivan*. There, Brennan J. held that public officials could only collect damages for statements concerning their fitness for office in circumstances where they could demonstrate that the defamatory statement was made "with knowledge that it was false or with reckless disregard of whether it was false or not."[56]

This example appears to confirm the general proposition that rules should be avoided that encourage large amounts of litigation, and thus discourage any activity that might trigger it—in this case, rules that create the substantial possibility of enormous payoffs. In my opinion, defamation law in Canada has an undesirable impact in the market of ideas and information. Libel chill is a real concern, especially for those engaged in political and social criticism. The deterrent impact of defamation law is not always signalled by an actual proliferation of lawsuits. The threat of litigation is sufficient in many cases. For example, there have been several high-profile examples of women complaining about sexism generally in the institutions where they work. They have not named individuals, nor given specific examples. They have been met with suits in defamation initiated by groups of men with whom they work. This is a very effective way to silence protest, even if success in court is not certain.

Insurance law

As noted above, in particular contexts liability regimes have such high transaction costs that they ought to be our last choice, if insurance is the primary goal. Fundamental tort reform includes the possibility of eliminating tort altogether in discrete areas where other insurance schemes are thought superior.[57]

No-fault automobile insurance

If victim compensation is the only goal, the transaction costs associated with auto-accident liability are wasteful. Of course, no-fault schemes are not perfect either. Victims may need to hire lawyers to secure the benefits to which they are entitled under first party no-fault. False claims are possibly more likely when litigation is by-passed. Nevertheless, no-fault remains far superior at putting premium dollars into the hands of legitimate accident victims. Every province in Canada has no-fault automobile insurance to some extent or another. Quebec and British Columbia, for example, have state-operated plans. Quebec alone in Canada has a pure (no residual tort liability) no-fault plan. Ontario's plan regulates no-fault cover provided by private insurers. It is a threshold plan, with access to tort allowed if the claim passes a statutory threshold. The plan changes with each new government.

Title insurance

It was noted at the outset that the partial Americanization of Canadian law was likely. The Americanization of Canadian business is inevitable. Title insurance companies based in the United States are aggressively seeking access to Canadian markets.[58] At present, in Ontario, for example, title insurance is only available after a lawyer has certified title. In other words, title insurance is effected through the lawyers' errors and omissions policy. (Title insurance is insurance against the possibility, given the frequently imperfect nature of real estate records, that creditors will turn out to have claims against a property that were undetected prior to the purchase.) Part of the fee for legal services is a component for title insurance. The title insurance companies believe they can offer a fully insured real estate transaction for much less than a lawyer would charge. I am not competent to judge whether consumers would lose out on other benefits of the legal service as lawyers claim, or whether rational consumers would want to purchase those benefits. But I can predict that the issue will prove to be a nasty one within the profession. The livelihood of much of the real estate bar is threatened directly by title insurance, and at a time where there seems to be underemployment in the profession generally. On the other hand, it may appeal to members of other segments of the bar who believe their errors and omissions premiums are subsidizing high-risk real estate practice.

The collateral source rule

The prevalent common law "collateral source" rule allows the plaintiff to recover in full from the tortfeasor, notwithstanding that the victim has already been, or will be, compensated for precisely the same losses by other sources such as employment benefits, private or government insurance. There are many statutory modifications to this rule, and a few tentative attempts to limit it at common law. Nevertheless, it remains the general common law rule.[59] Collateral sources may then recover the excess compensation received by the victim through a process known as subrogation. In practice, the typical lawsuit is waged by one or more insurers who cover the victim against another insurer who provides liability insurance to the defendant. By this process, society allows one company that has already spread the loss through underwriting to employ the high cost liability scheme to shift it to another company that will do the same thing. It is highly doubtful whether the deterrence incentives so obtained justify either double recovery when the collateral source finds it too expensive to pursue its right of subrogation, or the squandering of money due to redistribution of losses from one insurance pool to another when it does subrogate.

Conclusion

One certainly ought to be concerned about the question, "Are we seeing the tip of the iceberg in Canada?" given some of the horror stories that result from the question "What is going on in the United States?" My conclusion is that there is no real cause for concern in Canada about what is happening here, and indeed that concerns about importing American practice are largely misplaced because the general situation there is not nearly as bad as it may appear.[60] Moreover, most of the different patterns or outcomes that exist between the United States and Canada seem to have little to do with legal doctrine. Doctrine matters less than we think.

If one were to identify a single source of inefficiency in this area, it would be the liability system itself. It is too slow and expensive. It is necessary in some contexts to promote basic justice, and in others for deterrence. But on the whole, we need less of it, especially less negligence and strict liability. It is also the case that the openly pro-plaintiff bias in negligence law has generated more expensive liability than is really necessary, and considerable uncertainty. The practical consequences of this are probably more pronounced in commercial tort law than in personal injury law.

So, it is there that the attention of scholars, practitioners and reformers should be concentrated.

Acknowledgments

The author would like to thank the Faculty of Law and the Financial Aid Office of the University of Western Ontario for making it possible to engage the excellent research services of Stephanie Ross, Law III.

Notes

1 Thus references to Canadian tort law are to the law outside Quebec, although many similarities exist.

2 The duty of care in negligence law is the definition of the tortious obligation: e.g., the duty to take reasonable care to avoid causing personal injury; the duty to protect a child from harm; and so on. Indeed, one could argue that many significant changes to what was once governed exclusively by contract law have been achieved through new duties of care dealing with economic loss in tort. See generally B. Feldthusen, *Economic Negligence* (3d ed.), Toronto: Carswell, 1994.

3 [1977] 2 All E.R. 492 (H.L.) [hereinafter *Anns*].

4 I can think of only two recent Supreme Court of Canada decisions to have explicitly referred to the second branch of the *Anns* test. The cases were equally noteworthy because the Court actually held that

no duty of care existed. See *D'Amato* v. *Badger*, [1996] S.C.J. No. 84 (QL) and *Hercules Managements Ltd.* v. *Ernest and Young* [1997] S.C.J. No. 51 (QL). Whether they are harbingers of change, or merely specific responses to particular questions, remains to be seen. See generally, R. Kostal, "Liability For The Sale Of Alcohol: *Stewart* v. *Pettie*" (1996) 75 Can. Bar Rev. 169 at 175.

5 [1990] 3 W.L.R. 414 (H.L.).

6 It is often important for a defendant to have a case dismissed on a preliminary motion to a judge alone on the ground that the law does not recognize the duty of care that is the foundation of the plaintiff's claim. The idea is to have the judge dismiss the case before it is even tried because the facts alleged do not constitute a recognized legal wrong even if they did occur. Otherwise, the case may eventually go to a jury, and many defendants suspect juries of being pro-plaintiff and anti-corporate defendant.

7 See e.g., *CNR* v. *Norsk Pacific Steamship Co.*,[1992] 1 S.C.R. 1021, 91 D.L.R. (4th) 289; *Winnipeg Condominium Corp. #36* v. *Bird Construction Co.*, [1995] 1 S.C.R. 85.

8 See *supra* note 5.

9 B. Feldthusen, If This Is Torts, Negligence Must Be Dead, in K. Cooper-Stephenson and E. Gibson (eds.), *Tort Theory*, Toronto: Captus Press, 1993: 394.

10 See e.g., Brad Daisley, The Tug-of-War over Tobacco, *The Lawyers Weekly* (23 August 1991).

11 See J. Cassels, The Uncertain Promise of Law: Lessons From Bophal (1991) 29 Osgoode Hall L.J. 1.

12 See e.g., Monique Conrod, Undercompensation for Drug Injuries Common, Prof. Says." *The Lawyers Weekly* (13 January 1995).

13 See the discussion in the section "Malpractice," below.

14 See the rule in Bird Construction, discussed in the section "Municipal Liability," below.

15 B. Feldthusen and J. Palmer, *Winnipeg Condominium Corp. #36* v. *Bird Construction Co.*: Who Needs Contract Anymore? (1995) 25 Can. Bar Rev. 143.

16 The provinces are Quebec, British Columbia, and Ontario.

17 R. Posner, *Economic Analysis Of Law* (4th ed.), Toronto: Little, Brown, 1992: 137-9.

18 [1996] B.C.L.R. (3d) 144 (B.C. C.A.).

19 (1995), 128 D.L.R. (4th) 577 (B.C. S.C).

20 See Howard Burshtein, Plaintiffs Failed to Prove Fire Retardant Spray Was Health Hazard: B.C. Negligence Claim against Asbestos Product Fails," *The Lawyers Weekly* (8 December 1995).

21 *Deshane* v. *Deere & Co.*(1993), 15 O.R. (3d) 225, 106 D.L.R. (4th) 385 (C.A.), leave to ref'd. (1994), 110 D.L.R. (4th) vii (S.C.C.).

22 *Stiles* v. *Beckett, supra* note 17. See Teresa M. Dufort, ATV Ruling Suggests How Our Courts Will Approach Products Liability Cases. *The Lawyers Weekly* (16 April 1993).

23 [1995] 4 S.C.R. 634.

24 Cristin Schmitz, Heavy Burden Imposed on Manufacturers to Warn about Risk: S.C.C. Dismisses Breast Implant Appeal, *The Lawyers Weekly* (12 January 1996).

25 See generally, Brad Daisley, Time, Money, Good Claim Are Key to Malpractice Suit, *The Lawyers Weekly* (21 July 1995), quoting Maris McMillan.

26 [1982] S.C.R. 880.

27 [1990] 2 S.C.R. 320.

28 (1992), 12 C.C.L.T. (2d) 1 (S.C.C.).

29 *Supra* note 16.

30 J.R.S. Prichard, *Liability and Compensation in Health Care* (Toronto: University of Toronto Press, 1991).

31 Canada follows the leading English decision, *Hedley Byrne* v. *Heller*, [1964] A.C. 562 (H.L.). See especially *Haig* v. *Bamford* (1976), 72 D.L.R. (3d) 68 (S.C.C.). See generally, B. Feldthusen, *Economic Negligence, supra* note 2, chap. 2. I am also indebted to a paper prepared by Tom Heintzman, "Auditor's Liability," presented at the Court of Appeal for Ontario Annual Seminar, May 10, 1996.

32 Generally, liability in this area is premised on much the same principles expressed in S 552 of the Restatement of Torts (Second).

33 In *Haig* v. *Bamford, ibid.*, the court spoke of liability to a limited class. Contrast the leading English authority *Caparo Industries Plc.* v. *Dickman*, [1990] 1 All E.R. 568 (H.L.). Recently, the courts in Canada have taken a restrictive view, similar to the English. See *Hercules Management, supra* note 5.

34 Feldthusen, *Economic Negligence, supra* note 2, at 124.

35 See Heintzman, *supra* note 30.

36 The leading authority is *Anns* v. *London Borough of Merton, supra* note 3. In Canada, see especially *Kamloops* v. *Nielsen*, [1984] 2 S.C.R. 2, and *Just* v. *British Columbia*, [1989] 2 S.C.R. 1228.

37 See generally, B. Feldthusen, *Economic Negligence, supra* note 2, Chapter 6; Justice J. Sopinka, "The Liability of Public Authorities: Drawing The Line" (1993) 1 Tort L. Rev. 123. In two decisions subsequent to *Just*, *Brown* v. *British Columbia* (1994) 20 Admin. L.R. (2d) 1 (S.C.C.) and *Swinamer* v. *Nova Scotia* (1994) 20 Admin. L.R. (2d) 39 (S.C.C.), the court appeared to withdraw somewhat from the broad scope of liability contemplated in *Just*.

38 *Winnipeg Condominium Corp. #36* v. *Bird Construction Co., supra* note 6. Negligence liability for non-dangerous defects was left open, but seems unlikely.

39 B. Feldthusen and J. Palmer, *supra* note 14.
40 See the discussion in the section "Malpractice," above.
41 See the discussion in the section "Products Liability," above.
42 [1989] 2 S.C.R. 1181.
43 B. Feldthusen and N. Vidmar, "Exemplary damage Claims in Ontario: An Empirical Profile" (1990) 16 Can. Bus. L.J. 262.
44 I base this on a survey provided to the audience by Mr. Ian Binnie during a presentation on this topic at the Court of Appeal for Ontario Annual Seminar, May 10, 1996.
45 *Claiborne Industries* v. *National Bank of Canada* (1989), 69 O.R. (2d) 65 (C.A.).
46 *Whiten* v. *Pilot Insurance Co.* (1996), 132 D.L.R. (4th) 568 (Ont. Gen. Div.).
47 *Hill* v. *Church of Scientology of Toronto*, [1995] 2 S.C.R. 1130.
48 See *A.(B.)* v. *I.(J.)*, [1991] 5 W.W.R. 748 (Alta. Q.B.); *B.(P.)* v. *B.(W.)* (1992), 11 O.R. (3d) 161 (Gen. Div.); *P.C.P.* v. *Da Costa*, [1992] B.C.J. No. 2303 (QL)(B.C. S.C.); *S.C.* v. *R.L.L.* (1993), 133 N.B.R. (2d) 332 (Q.B.); and *Q.(S.M.)* v. *Hodgins* (1991), 36 R.F.L. (3d) 159 (Ont. Gen. Div.).
49 *Lubrizol Corp.* v. *Imperial Oil* (1994), 84 F.T.R. 197 (T.D.).
50 It was also a significant factor in the award in *Whiten, supra* note 44.
51 (1996), 67 C.P.R. (3d) 1 (F.C.A.). The matter was returned to trial to consider whether the conduct truly met the threshold for punitive damages.
52 *Vorvis* v. *Insurance Corporation of British Columbia*, [1989] 1 S.C.R. 1085.
53 See B. Feldthusen, "Punitive Damages In Canada: Can the Coffee Ever Be Too Hot" (1995) 17 Loyola of L.A. International & Comparative L.J. 793.
54 *Hill* v. *Church of Scientology of Toronto, supra* note 45.
55 Personal injury general damages are capped at $100,000 in 1978 dollars, or approximately $250,000 today. See *Andrews* v. *Grand & Toy (Alta.) Ltd.*, [1978] 2 S.C.R. 229.
56 376 U.S. 254, 280 (1964).
57 I do not mean to suggest that tort is or ought to be only, or even mainly, an insurance scheme. Proper evaluation must take other goals, notably corrective justice and deterrence, into account.
58 See Bob Aaron, Title Insurance Poses Threat to Ont. Registry System, *The Lawyers Weekly* (1 December 1995); Title Insurance Is Changing Real Estate Practice: Bar, Insurers Are Lining Up to Do Battle, *The Lawyers Weekly* (5 July 1996).
59 See *Ratych* v. *Bloomer* (1990), 3 C.C.L.T. (2d) 1 (S.C.C.); and *Cunningham* v. *Wheeler*, [1994] 1 S.C.R. 359.
60 See Ontario Law Reform Commission, *Report on Exemplary Damages* (Toronto, 1990).

Table of cases

A.(B.) v. *I.(J.)*, [1991] 5 W.W.R. 748 (Alta. Q.B.).
Andrews v. *Grand & Toy (Alta.) Ltd.*, [1978] 2 S.C.R. 229.
Anns v. *London Borough of Merton*, [1977] 2 All E.R. 492 (H.L.).
B.(P.) v. *B.(W.)* (1992), 11 O.R. (3d) 161 (Gen. Div.).
Brown v. *British Columbia* (1994) 20 Admin. L.R. (2d) 1 (S.C.C.).
Caparo Industries Plc. v. *Dickman*, [1990] 1 All E.R. 568 (H.L.).
Claiborne Industries v. *National Bank of Canada* (1989), 69 O.R. (2d) 65 (C.A.).
C.N.R. v. *Norsk Pacific Steamship Co.*, [1992] 1 S.C.R. 1021.
D'Amato v. *Badger*, [1996] S.C.J. No. 84 (QL).
Deshane v. *Deere & Co.* (1993), 15 O.R. (3d) 225 (C.A.).
Haig v. *Bamford* (1976), 72 D.L.R. (3d) 68 (S.C.C.).
Hedley Byrne v. *Heller*, [1964] A.C. 562 (H.L.).
Hercules Managements Ltd. v. *Ernest and Young* [1997] S.C.J. No. 51 (QL)
Hill v. *Church of Scientology of Toronto*, [1995] 2 S.C.R. 1130.
Hollis v. *Dow Corning*, [1995] 4 S.C.R. 634.
Just v. *British Columbia*, [1989] 2 S.C.R. 1228.
Kamploops v. *Nielsen*, [1984] 2 S.C.R. 2.
Lubrizol Corp. v. *Imperial Oil* (1994), 84 F.T.R. 197 (T.D.), rev'd (1996), 67 C.P.R. (3d) 1 (F.C.A.).
Murphy v. *Brentwood District Council*, [1990] 3 W.L.R. 414 (H.L.).
New York Times Co. v. *Sullivan*, 376 U.S. 254, 280 (1964).
Norberg v. *Wynrib* (1992), 12 C.C.L.T. (2d) 1 (S.C.C.).
P.C.P. v. *DaCosta*, [1992] B.C.J. No. 2303 (QL)(S.C.).
Privest Properties Ltd. v. *W.R. Grace & Co. of Canada Ltd.* (1995), 128 D.L.R. (4th) 577 (B.C. S.C.).
Q.(S.M.) v. *Hodgins* (1991), 36 R.F.L. (3d) 159 (Ont. Gen. Div.).
Ratych v. *Bloomer* (1990), 3 C.C.L.T. (2d) 1 (S.C.C.).
Reibl v. *Hughes*, [1982] S.C.R. 880.
S.C. v. *R.L.L.* (1993), 133 N.B.R. (2d) 332 (Q.B.).
Snell v. *Farrell*, [1990] 2 S.C.R. 320.
Stiles v. *Beckett*, [1996] B.C.L.R. (3d) 144 (C.A.).
Swinamer v. *Nova Scotia* (1994), 20 Admin. L.R. (2d) 39 (S.C.C.).
Tock v. *St. John Metropolitan Area Board*, [1989] 2 S.C.R. 1181.
Vorvis v. *Insurance Corporation of British Columbia*, [1989] 1 S.C.R. 1085.
Whiten v. *Pilot Insurance Co.* (1996), 132 D.L.R. (4th) 568 (Ont. Gen. Div.).
Winnipeg Condominium Corp. #36 v. *Bird Construction Co.*, [1995] 1 S.C.R. 85.

Selected references

Aaron, B. Title Insurance Poses Threat to Ont. Registry System, *The Lawyers Weekly* (1 December 1995).

——— Title Insurance Is Changing Real Estate Practice: Bar, Insurers Are Lining Up to Do Battle, *The Lawyers Weekly* (5 July 1996).

Brown, C. *No-Fault Automobile Insurance in Canada.* Toronto: Carswell, 1988.

Burshtein, H. Plaintiffs Failed to Prove Fire Retardant Spray Was Health Hazard: B.C. Negligence Claim against Asbestos Product Fails, *The Lawyers Weekly* (8 December 1995).

Cassels, J. The Uncertain Promise of Law: Lessons from Bophal (1991) 29 Osgoode Hall L.J. 1

Conrod, M. Undercompensation for Drug Injuries Common, Prof. Says, *The Lawyers Weekly* (13 January 1995).

Daisley, B. The Tug-of-War over Tobacco, *The Lawyers Weekly* (23 August 1991).

——— Time, Money, Good Claim Are Key to Malpractice Suit, *The Lawyers Weekly* (21 July 1995).

Dufort, T.M. ATV Ruling Suggests How Our Courts Will Approach Products Liability Cases, *The Lawyers Weekly* (16 April 1993).

Feldthusen, B. *Economic Negligence* (3rd ed.). Toronto: Carswell, 1994.

——— If This Is Torts, Negligence Must Be Dead. In K. Cooper-Stephenson and E. Gibson (eds.), *Tort Theory* (Toronto: Captus Press, 1993).

——— Punitive Damages in Canada: Can the Coffee Ever Be too Hot (1995), Loyola of L.A. International and Comparative L.J. 793.

Feldthusen, B. and Palmer, J. *Winnipeg Condominium Corp. #36* v. *Bird Construction Co.*: Who Needs Contract Anymore? (1995) 25 Can. Bar Rev. 143.

Feldthusen, B. and Vidmar, N. Exemplary Damage Claims in Ontario: An Empirical Profile: (1990) 16 Can. Bus. L.J. 262.

Heintzman, T. Auditors Liability (paper presented at Court of Appeal for Ontario Annual Seminar, 1996).

Kostal, R. Liability For the Sale of Alcohol: *Stewart* v. *Pettie* (1996) 75 Can. Bar Rev. 169.

Prichard, J.R.S. *Liability and Compensation in Health Care.* Toronto: University of Toronto Press, 1991.

Schmitz, C. Heavy Burden Imposed on Manufacturers to Warn About Risk: S.C.C. Dismisses Breast Implant Appeal, *The Lawyers Weekly* (12 January 1996).

Sopinka, J. The Liability of Public Authorities: Drawing the Line, (1993) 1 Tort L.R. 123.

Civil Justice Reform in Ontario

CHARLES HARNICK

A litigation explosion in Ontario

Whether or not Canada is inheriting America's litigious legacy, there can be no question that Ontario has already experienced a litigation explosion. In the past decade, more than 1.8 million civil cases were filed in Ontario courts. Ontario courts hear almost one-third of the country's civil suits, the most of any jurisdiction in Canada (though, since it accounts for well over one-third of Canada's population and of its GDP, this figure is if anything lower than one might expect). And, whatever one may say about its fundamental causes and cures, this explosion presents an immediate problem for which immediate solutions must be found. As things stand, parties can wait up to five years before their case is heard. That has led to exorbitant costs to litigants. Delays and high costs are a recipe for disaster for those who need our courts to settle their disputes.

Our challenge as administrators of the system is to deal with the consequences of the explosion that has already occurred and prevent such things from happening again. We must improve

Note will be found on page 114.

the justice system and develop a more accessible, affordable and efficient civil justice system for all Ontarians.

The need for such a system is obvious. Businesses, investors and individuals—those who create jobs and prosperity—need a civil justice system that works with them, not against them. When looking for places to invest their capital and create jobs, corporations need to know that they will be able to settle their commercial disputes with reasonable costs and minimal inconvenience. Entrepreneurs and risk takers value doing business in locations that can deliver swift and effective justice. Quick resolution of disputes is in everyone's best interest. It is good for business, individuals and the province's economy. It is clear that, whatever the underlying benefits or costs of various types of litigation under various legal rules, a system that does not deal expeditiously with those cases that do arise is failing the community.

Current problems

As a former civil litigator, I have experienced at first hand the problems in the civil justice system. Let me outline them. In a nutshell, Ontario's civil justice system undermines our competitiveness with slow, costly, inefficient and outdated services.

The system is slow We know the system is slow, because the average civil case takes five years to settle. Even after all of the preparation is done and the case is ready to go to trial, it can take a year-and-a-half to get into court. The toll this takes on a company, its employees and individual litigants is enormous. Employees and managers spend their time in meetings preparing for trial, rather than on the shop floor ensuring the success and survival of the business. Their time is better spent producing goods and services rather than giving depositions. Goods and services add to our economic growth. Depositions do not.

The system is costly We know the system is costly because on average, a typical litigant in a civil action that goes to trial spends about $38,000 just in lawyer's fees to recover $55,000. I personally have seen the financial drain that the civil justice system imposes upon businesses and individuals. It is not a pretty sight.

The system is inefficient We know the system is inefficient because 96 percent of civil actions settle before they go to trial. In all but a small minority of cases, then, it is in the perceived interest of neither party to have the case run the gamut of the court process. However, the civil justice system fails adequately to reflect that fact in the way cases are handled. The system is geared to bring cases to trial, as opposed to developing mechanisms to help parties settle at an earlier stage of the process.

The system is outdated It is no secret that our justice system is outdated. In an era where computers and the Internet dominate our culture, our civil justice system still operates in the quill and paper era of the nineteenth century. It is paper driven to the point that we spend more than $8 million per year storing legal briefs that few people ever read.

Solutions

Our civil justice system has been taken for granted. It is a labour intensive system that lacks technology. This must end. It is time to adopt the tools of the twenty-first century, because we have missed the twentieth.

There have been many studies about the civil justice system. One of those is the Civil Justice Review, which has now issued two reports on how to improve the justice system. The Civil Justice Review is important because it included representation from the public, lawyers, judges and ministry officials. The parties involved set aside their vested interests and have proposed a number of practical, results-oriented solutions to improve our civil courts. I am a strong proponent of their work and have begun implementing their recommendations.

Clearing the backlog

The first step we have taken is to eliminate the backlogs in our civil courts. The backlog of civil cases in Ontario awaiting disposition has been steadily increasing for decades. A year ago it was five times larger than it was in 1975. We have eliminated the backlogs by blitzing specific areas and finding quicker and less costly ways of resolving cases. Now, thanks to the work of judges and lawyers, that delay has been all but wiped out. Lawyers, in particular, have provided thousands of voluntary hours tackling court lists and conducting pre-trial conferences.

Case management

We are building on these gains by implementing key recommendations contained in the Civil Justice Review, which will avoid renewed backlogs. One of the first steps we are taking is expanding case management across the province to ensure cases are heard quickly. Case management puts responsibility for the progress of a case in the hands of judges, rather than lawyers acting for the opposing parties. Case management rules set strict deadlines to which lawyers must adhere. Penalties are in place for those who fail to meet the deadlines. The experience of pilot projects in Ontario and extensive experience in other jurisdictions show that case management reduces delay in civil courts and reduces costs to litigants. By the start of next year, we will have case management in place for 100 percent of the civil cases in Ottawa and from 25 to 50 percent of the cases in Toronto.

To ensure that case management succeeds, we are bringing back the Office of the Master. The new Case Management Master will provide the necessary support to judges for the expansion of civil case management. By employing a team approach, we will move lawsuits through the system quickly and affordably.

Alternative dispute resolution

We will also expand the use of mediation in the civil process because we know it works. The ADR pilot project in Toronto showed that as many as 40 percent of cases can be settled by mediation *before* they reach the discovery stage. That suggests enormous savings in time and costs and less emotional turmoil for litigants. I am committed to implementing mandatory referral to mediation in non-family, civil disputes. While the details must still be worked out, I believe the best way to employ mediation would be through a system where private sector mediators are available to mediate cases. Cases where mediation fails or is inappropriate will be able to continue down the traditional court path.

Simpler rules for small cases

We have also instituted simpler rules for cases involving less than $25,000. The Rules eliminate the need for the costly discovery process. We are now considering if these simplified rules should be extended to cases involving as much as $50,000. The alternative is to increase monetary caps at the Small Claim Courts, where parties do not need to hire lawyers to represent themselves.

We know that the justice system can operate without the complicated process of discovery. Labour tribunals, for example, have been operating effectively for years without the use of discoveries. They have been successful in resolving disputes where often much more than $25,000 is at stake.

New technology

Changing the way we handle cases is only one part of our strategy to improve the civil justice system. Another key component involves introducing new technology to our court system. As suggested by the Civil Justice Review, the efficient use of information technology must play a key role in reforming the civil justice system. The process is under way. We have provided the software necessary to Toronto and Ottawa to support case management.

We have also been experimenting with electronic filing of lawsuits. This system will allow parties to file documents with the courts electronically and will eliminate many of the line-ups that plague the courts in Toronto. A pilot will begin in Toronto in August 1997 in which filing statements of claim and defence will be done electronically: approximately 100 firms of all sizes will participate in the project, which will be evaluated after six months. Electronic filing will revolutionize the administration of justice. It will improve the efficiency of our courts by linking them directly to law offices. Why should the courts be a repository for documents that can be held by parties? But this is a very modest first step; much larger changes are in the works.

In August 1996, the ministry of the Attorney General and the ministry of the Solicitor General and Correctional Services issued a joint request for proposals on the development of technological solutions to integrate the sharing of information among authorized users in the justice system. This project is intended to provide tools for all parts of the justice system—including police, prosecutors, civil and criminal courts, Ontario Board of Parole, correctional institutions, and probation and parole services—to support the efficient delivery of justice services. Obviously, this is a costly exercise and one that is difficult to undertake when you have an accumulated debt of almost $100 billion and a deficit of almost $9 billion. We believe, however, that we can achieve our goal of modernizing the justice system by developing technological solutions with the private sector. The private sector partner would be paid out of the efficiencies new business processes and enabling technology will bring to the justice system. The savings are enormous. By working with twenty-first century technology and processes, we will truly be able to do better for less.

Conclusion: long-term prospects

In conclusion, I am confident that we have taken the necessary steps to deal with the explosion in litigation that has already occurred in Ontario. But looking further ahead, my view from the inside is that it is safe to say that Ontario—and Canada—will not experience the litigation frenzy currently underway south of the border.

I believe that for a couple of reasons. First, we already have the best deterrent to excessive litigiousness that can exist in a civilized justice system—our "loser-pays" system. When the losing party pays a portion of the legal fees to the winner, it deters pointless or malicious litigation.

Second, we already have class action legislation and limited contingency fees, but in a form that does not lend itself to frivolous actions. Access to funding for class action litigation is minimal. The funding pool is $500,000. Certainly thus far there has not been an explosion of this type of litigation in Ontario.[1]

I think that we are well on our way to bringing administration and management of the current volume of cases in this province properly under control. The changes I have outlined will improve the administration of justice and provide greater access to the justice system for a much larger number of Ontarians. It will improve the climate for investment and provide businesses with timely resolution of their disputes.

Adapting to these changes will present challenges to some parts of the profession and I have no wish to minimize or belittle the difficulties some will face.

But with hard work, creative thinking, and commitment on the part of our justice system partners, I am confident that we can build a more responsive, accessible, affordable and efficient civil justice system—a system that meets the needs of individuals and one that encourages companies to consider Ontario as a place to invest.

Note

1 See also the chapter by S. Gordon McKee, this volume, for a more thorough discussion of class action legislation and prospects in Canada.

Is Canada Inheriting America's Litigious Legacy?

ROY MCMURTRY

Cause for concern

The subject of whether Canada is inheriting America's litigious legacy, or for that matter developing one independently, is most important. My area of expertise is Ontario so my presentation tries to give a brief overview in relation to the many challenges facing the civil justice system in an Ontario context. However, many discussions with my fellow chief justices would suggest that the challenges are remarkably similar in the most populous provinces of Canada.

The distressing reality is that the civil justice system in Ontario has in recent years increasingly failed to provide a dispute resolution system that operates in a timely and affordable way for the majority of our fellow citizens. The malaise is deep and so it is immensely important that we take a hard collective look at its problems and potential solutions.

Just another social program

Having served as the attorney general for Ontario for a decade, I have been long aware of the lack of a broadly based political constituency for the civil justice system. Responsible people have traditionally supported the concept of an effective, accessible justice system in the abstract, but for the majority it was somebody else's problem and they have given little thought or effort to making the system work. Most people do not expect ever to be in a courtroom, and until they or someone close to them gets caught up in the process of civil litigation, it is clearly not something they think about very much. The result is that the constituency most interested in the civil justice system, at least until recently, has very seldom appeared to extend very far beyond the ranks of the legal profession and the judiciary. The unfortunate perception of a relatively small, special-interest group in support of the civil justice system for their own purposes has had, and still has, profound implications for attorneys general in their struggles to adequately fund the justice system in an age of shrinking government resources.

While lip service is paid by governments to the importance of the justice system, when it actually comes to allocating funds, however, their priorities are elsewhere. There is certainly no mystery about this reality, as every citizen is affected by the quality of health, education, social services, highways and so on, but does not expect to get caught up in the justice system.

There is also often an attitude within government that the justice system is just another social service program. Coupled with this is the additional fact that many within government see the justice system as rather an exclusive club of lawyers and judges that has traditionally shunned efficiencies as incompatible with justice.

The message that chief justices must continuously bring to government, therefore, is that the justice system is not just one more "social service" program, but it is rather a foundation stone upon which a civil and caring society is built. Too often the justice system is taken for granted, but if it deteriorates, we all suffer.

How to improve the system

The necessity of adequate resources is therefore a fundamental issue that must be addressed if there is to be meaningful reform of the civil justice system.

Personnel

One common element of every recent study of court systems in Canada is the shared recognition of the need for a cadre of professional court administrators and an effective management structure. In my view any discussion of civil justice reform should include a recognition of this need. This is not to suggest that such persons do not already serve the justice system, but the experience in Ontario and elsewhere has been decidedly mixed. Effective courts administration also requires a technological infrastructure to bring the court systems into the twentieth century, preferably before we enter the twenty-first century. It is not an exaggeration to state that many of our court offices have not progressed beyond the pen and quill methods of the nineteenth century. Many documents have to be laboriously recorded by hand before being stuffed into files which lack adequate storage and are frequently lost. In Toronto a law firm process clerk may have to wait for hours to be served in some of the court offices.

In my experience, an effective administration of the court system involves both science and art, and we should not overemphasize technology. While a technological infrastructure will go a long way towards the development of more effective courts administration, trained and experienced court administrators are essential.

A court services agency

I am in total support of the concept of a court services agency, described elsewhere in this volume by Ontario's Attorney General, as this has the potential to provide a combination of a more professional administration and a greater accountability to the public.

Case management

A major part of the solution is effective case management. The cost of civil litigation is directly related to the period of time during which a dispute is being litigated. Pilot projects in Toronto and elsewhere have demonstrated that case management by judges can halve the average time taken for the resolution of a civil dispute.

Case management is a relatively new initiative in Canada and it simply means earlier judicial intervention. It was initially resisted by many judges in Canada who saw their role as restricted to trying cases in the court room rather than helping them get there in a timely fashion. However, the concept of case management is now accepted by the judiciary, who endorsed the first report of the Ontario justice review that said:

> It must operate under the model of caseflow management, a time and event management system which facilitates early resolution of cases, reduces delays and back-logs and lowers the cost of litigation. Caseflow management shifts the overall management of cases through time parameters from the bar ... where it has traditionally been ... to the judiciary, streamlines the process, permits the introduction of ADR techniques, and creates an environment where judges, administrators, and quasi-judicial officials can work together to integrate the various elements of the system into a co-ordinated whole.

As Attorney General Charles Harnick states in Civil Justice Reform in Ontario (this volume), he too is strongly in support of case management and the other important recommendations of the civil justice review, including of course the currently very popular concept of alternate dispute resolution (ADR). My preference is for a form of court-annexed ADR if the ordinary litigant is going to be able to have a more timely and affordable resolution of civil disputes.

The case for improving the system

Making the court system work better enhances not only justice today but also opportunity tomorrow. Very simply, too much litigation and litigation that moves too slowly divert energy and imagination away from wealth creation into useless or downright harmful activities. The experiences described by other contributors to this book have focused on the deleterious effects of the litigation explosion in the United States in the context of large corporations, but everyone recognizes the vital role of the small business community in relation to a healthy economy and small businesses are much less able to bear the costs of interminable litigation. Indeed, there are thousands of small business people in particular in Ontario who believe that they are effectively shut out of the court system because of the cost.

However, the reduction of the cost of litigation that can be accomplished by following the recommendations of the Ontario civil justice review does do have some significant financial implications for a government that is committed to deficit reduction. The current government jargon is that everyone who spends public funds must make a business case for their expenditure. And the business case for civil justice is very simple.

Society simply cannot function without a system that allows people to have their disputes resolved and determined in an orderly and effective fashion. The alternative is civil chaos and perhaps even violence. A stable civil justice system is also a critical underpinning for business and commerce, domestic and international.

The cost of civil justice in Ontario is more than recovered in court fees. Under the present budgetary process, the ministries of the Attorney General in Ontario and other provinces do not receive credit for the revenues that are produced in the administration of the courts. This policy must be changed if there is to be a meaningful dialogue among those involved in the administration of justice as to what improvements can be made available on the basis of some cost recovery.

But in any case the social gain from effective and efficient dispute resolution is far greater than court fees alone would suggest. The business case for civil justice would emphasizes not only its lack of direct cost to the provincial treasury, but also its central role in protecting our economic infrastructure and the gains we derive from it. Recent experience in other countries, including parts of the former Soviet Union, shows that the disintegration of the legal system cripples the economy. No one, foreigner or even resident, will invest much in a country or a province that lacks the basic capacity to resolve commercial disputes in a timely, effective, and predictable fashion. Conversely, recent experience shows that effective court systems, such as the British commercial court, attract business and stimulate the economy.

Unfortunately our provincial and federal governments lack the capacity to analyze and to measure court and judicial workload, effectiveness, and productivity in a way that makes possible the development of a solid business case for civil justice. We do not even have court statistical systems that produce meaningful workload indicators. This again underlines the importance of a specialized court services agency.

Conclusion: not just another social program

In conclusion, this description by the Ontario law reform commission in 1973 of the role of the courts in our system of government is equally apt today.

> The basic function of a court system in a civilized society is the impartial adjudication of disputes without resort to violence. As part of the institutional framework for the peaceful settlement of conflicting interests, the courts of law stand at the pivotal point of the scales of justice, ready to apply the rule of law to the issue between the parties coming before them. Thus, they represent the substitution of the authoritative power of reason, knowledge, wisdom and experience for the naked power of force.

It is my hope that all Canadians will realize the importance of focusing governments' attention upon the vital importance of the civil justice system to an orderly, civil, and prosperous society.

Canadian Economic Regulation

Balancing Efficiency and Fair Process

KONRAD VON FINCKENSTEIN†

A balance of efficiency and fairness

It is my contention that the future development of Canadian regulatory regimes should proceed in precisely the direction that we have been going over the last 15 to 20 years—right down the middle of the road between the political and economic objective of regulatory efficiency on the one hand and the legal protection of fairness and natural justice on the other—what Americans usually refer to as "due process of law." Coming as they do from one who is fundamentally a commercial and trade lawyer, my remarks are focused on the impact of American legal trends as they pertain to *economic* regulation under Canadian federal law.

Canadian federal law has achieved quite a good balance between regulatory efficiency and due process. Regulation of any kind, whether in aid of economic, social, environmental, or cultural objectives, imposes costs on both regulator and regulatee. The cost to regulated industries is tied up in a host of things,

† The views expressed here are those of the author and not of the Department of Justice or the Federal Government.

including outlays for accommodating regulatory processes, delays in obtaining regulatory approvals for business ventures, and the cost of licence fees. Obviously regulatory efficiency is desirable to keep those costs down to the lowest feasible level without undermining the integrity of the regulatory process. And Canada has seen remarkable progress in terms of efficiency. Ten or fifteen years ago, it was not unusual for public hearings by the Canadian Radio-television and Telecommunications Commission (CRTC) into rates increases for telephone companies to last 6 weeks, even 8 or 10 weeks in some instances. Today, with increased competition, there is a substantially diminished need for rate regulation to begin with and what regulatory approval still is required for telephone rates now typically takes 5 to 8 *days*.

At the same time, our legal system—principally our system of administrative law—has imposed substantive and procedural fairness on ministers, public servants, and administrative tribunals in respect of the regulatory functions they perform. Because of forward-looking decisions of the Supreme Court of Canada in the late 1970s and 1980s, administrative decision-making has been demystified, allowing the rules of natural justice and procedural fairness to apply to virtually all decisions made by public authorities in Canada. There are also particular statutory regimes that enhance both regulatory efficiency and due process in specific areas. By focusing on four significant examples, I hope to demonstrate that, whether by accident or design or both, we have fashioned a pretty good regulatory system that serves our needs well. It is a system that we should continually try to perfect, but that is not in need of a radical overhaul. The components contributing to the balance in our regulatory system come from British, European, and American legal and regulatory influences that we have had the good sense to adopt and adapt to suit our own particular political and economic needs.

Four examples of good balance

The four examples used to support this thesis are drawn from diverse areas of commercial and economic activity and responsibility. They are (1) the regulation of broadcasting by the CRTC; (2) the government procurement review system; (3) competition regulation falling under the director of Investigation and Research; and, (4) the supervision of trustees in bankruptcy by the superintendent of Bankruptcy. These examples are chosen because, in addition to being relevant and representative, they also fall within the business portfolio of the department of Justice for which I am responsible and are, therefore, instances about which I have some knowledge.

Broadcasting regulation

Broadcasting regulation is an appropriate place to start because the Canadian Radio-television and Telecommunications Commission (CRTC) is probably the best known of Canada's federal regulatory agencies. Its mandate takes it into some of the most contentious areas of Canadian public policy and public interest: economic regulation of telecommunications, related social and cultural matters, as well as the economic regulation of broadcasting itself. Since 98 percent of Canadian households have telephone service, 99 percent have television and 75 percent subscribe to cable, its decisions are directly felt by virtually all members of Canadian society.

Like its American counterpart, the Federal Communications Commission (FCC), the CRTC wears two hats—a telecommunications hat and a broadcasting hat. Unlike the FCC, however, the CRTC's hats have fundamentally different shapes. Its telecommunications regulatory mandate has essentially shifted from strict economic rate-of-return regulation of telecommunications carriers to regulation of competition among service providers. On the broadcasting side, however, its mandate has remained essentially unchanged: licensing and regulation of broadcasting undertakings to achieve social, cultural, and political objectives defined in the statutory broadcasting policy enunciated by Parliament. Because the overwhelming number of the actual players within the Canadian broadcasting system are private entities pursuing commercial interests, the CRTC cannot help being controversial in many of the decisions it issues. My concern here is not with specific high-profile CRTC decisions but rather, with the routine operations of the regulatory system itself.

The heart and soul of CRTC broadcasting regulation is the process of public hearings, not only in relation to the issuance and renewal or amendment of broadcasting licences, but also in relation to regulation-making. For example, recently the CRTC held public hearings on proposed new regulations for cable. As the name implies, it is a public and transparent process with fairly strict and straight-forward rules governing how it is to be conducted.

There is no concern that I am aware of as to the sufficiency of due process regarding the CRTC's broadcasting licensing powers—the public hearing model and administrative tribunal status of the CRTC assure plenty of due process there. It is an independent body whose members having security of tenure. The CRTC jealously guards its independence, which is exactly what it should do. To preserve that independence while ensuring that it fulfils its legitimate mandate, Parliament created two extraordinary legal means to ensure that the CRTC would implement the statutory objectives for broadcasting that Parliament itself had set out in s.3 of the *Broadcasting Act*.

On one hand, it gave Cabinet, acting through the legal fiction of the Governor in Council, the power to issue "policy directions" to the CRTC subject to the caveat that such directions must be on broad policy matters of general application, and made sure that the process of giving policy directions would be transparent by requiring that, before a direction is given, the CRTC be consulted and that the direction be tabled in Parliament, where it may be debated. The second thing that Parliament did was to give the Cabinet the authority to review licensing decisions issued by the CRTC in the light of whether or not any such decision derogates from the attainment of the broadcasting policy set out in the *Broadcasting Act*.

An unwritten principle governing these extraordinary powers is that they be used sparingly, which has, in fact, been the case. In the 5 years since the power of policy direction has been in place, only one "policy direction" has been issued, that dealing with Direct-to-Home satellite television broadcasting. And out of the thousands of licensing decisions made annually, fewer than a handful, typically not even a dozen, have been set aside or referred back for reconsideration by Cabinet in any given year. So, when you factor in the quality or survival rate of the CRTC's decisions and the Governor in Council (Cabinet)'s praiseworthy self-restraint respecting its extraordinary powers, this is an excellent example of a truly Canadian regulatory solution to balancing regulatory efficiency and due process. It balances the due process of the American model, which lacks a mechanism for direct input of policy implementation, with the direct input of some European models that lack the transparency and due process inherent in our model, even though they have transformed their broadcasting systems from exclusive state-run systems into mixed systems with public and private components.

Government procurement

The current regime regarding government procurement is quite new. It was only in 1989 as part of the Canada/United States Free Trade Agreement that Canada adopted a government procurement review system by an independent adjudicative entity. Unlike the American system, however, in which there are several procurement review boards, each functioning separately and, to all intents and purposes, as courts of first instance, Parliament took the more economical route of adopting one-stop shopping at the Canadian International Trade Tribunal (CITT).

The process put in place for government procurement encompasses the usual requirements for contracts above a certain dollar level to be granted by public tendering, followed by objective evaluation of bids received in accordance with neutral, published criteria. Potential suppliers of goods and services to the government have recourse to the CITT by virtue of the North American Free Trade Agreement (NAFTA), the World Trade Organization (WTO) Agreement and the interprovincial Agreement on Internal Trade, all of which set out standards that have to be observed in the tendering process. If someone who unsuccessfully tendered a bid to supply the federal government with goods or services is dissatisfied with the decision that was made, they may ask the CITT to review the tender, and the CITT's potential remedies include the award of a contract if the complaint is filed within 10 days of the decision it concerns. In fact, even before a contract is awarded, a potential supplier can file a complaint to the CITT on a variety of grounds including, for example, unfair or unreasonable technical specifications or exclusion from the tender process itself.

Once a complaint has been received, the CITT receives submissions from all parties and conducts its own investigation, which may include the holding of a public hearing. The investigation, in any case, is conducted in an open and transparent manner. At the end of this process, if the CITT believes that the complaint is valid, it will issue a recommendation to the relevant government institution. If the complaint is upheld, the CITT can recommend that the contract award be cancelled and retendering take place, or that the award be upheld but that some other remedy be implemented. In disposing of a complaint, the CITT can award bid preparation costs and/or costs associated with the bringing of the complaint itself. In addition, unlike its American counterparts, the CITT *can* award compensation for such injuries as loss of profits.

The decision of the CITT is only a recommendation. It does not bind the Crown. However, the government institution is admonished to implement the recommendation "to the extent possible" and, though it can choose to ignore the recommendation, the general scheme of procurement review envisaged by Parliament makes it clear that the CITT's recommendations are to be implemented except under exceptional circumstances.

If the complaining contractor is a foreign contractor there may be international trade law consequences and, in that case, the procuring entity can choose between judicial or political accountability. Not surprisingly, they have mostly chosen the former. However, the latter is an escape valve available to avoid implementing an unreasonable or patently impracticable decision. Again we have a balance between fairness and efficiency or, in this case, practicality.

Competition

The third example, competition law, is obviously vital to the operation of a healthy economy. Different countries take different approaches to ensuring and enforcing fair competition, with no one model necessarily better than another and no single model inherently suitable to all states and all economies. But it is important to have one that is suitable to one's own situation, and that is well designed.

The American anti-trust model contains *per se* offences and also allows the awarding of triple damages to injured parties. It has become a major cost factor for business and a significant source of complaint. A major source of trouble under this regime is that although the government can and does bring anti-trust suits against companies engaged in price fixing, predatory pricing, or other anti-competitive practices, treble damages are available to private litigants.

Perhaps the American system is appropriate for a domestic market that is equivalent in size to a continental economy. It is doubtful, however, whether the full American treble-damage model would be suitable or beneficial to Canada. And I hold this view notwithstanding the fact that a similar, albeit more limited, private remedy is available in Canada. For here in Canada, with a smaller marketplace and historically greater reliance on public authority to enforce public law, we have created a director of Investigation and Research as the central figure in competition regulation.

The director of Investigation and Research is appointed by the Governor in Council and while he is a member of the department of Industry's executive, he is totally independent in terms of his enforcement activities. All complaints of anti-competitive practices must go through him. He investigates independently and is the only person that can (a) make a recommendation to the Attorney General for prosecutions in respect of criminal anti-competitive conduct, such as price fixing or (b) decide to take companies before the Competition Tribunal for civilly reviewable competitive conduct, such as mergers that will lessen competition.

For most practical purposes, by taking the initiative for commencing criminal prosecutions and civil proceedings for competition violations out of the hands of private parties, we have protected Canadian businesses from the constant threat of litigation that is possible under American law. This balance between public and private interest is reinforced by the fact that the director of Investigation and Research is not vested with enormous, unrestrained powers. He cannot himself prosecute. He can only investigate and make recommendations to the Attorney General. Nor can he simply ignore complaints. He must inquire when so requested by six persons no matter who they are, as well as when directed to do so by the Minister. As a result, Canada has a vigorous competition enforcement model without the tremendous cost and delays involved in the United States. Here again Canada has a struck a good and unique balance.

Bankruptcy

Under our system, in the event of a bankruptcy a trustee is appointed by the official receiver, a court officer, to administer the estate of an insolvent person or company whether for the purpose of rehabilitation or liquidation. A trustee has heavy fiduciary responsibilities and may have administration of significant assets. Judicial intervention to superintend the functioning of a trustee is limited and, in some measure, depends upon the trustee himself seeking judicial authorization pertaining to acts of administration of estates under his care. Accordingly, the essence of our entire regime is to select trustees who are themselves trustworthy and who will do the job required of them in a professional and dispassionate manner.

It is therefore on the initial selection of trustees that our regulatory system concentrates. The key player in all of this is the superintendent of Bankruptcy. His functions are to license trustees, to set professional standards and to discipline trustees where required. The superintendent, as an Order-in-Council appointee with specific statutory functions, enjoys, as does the director in Canada's anti-trust system, considerable independence. However, he or she is also a member of the department of Industry and reports to an assistant deputy minister of the Department.

As for the system of supervision, where there is reason to believe, whether because of complaints about a trustee or because of the results of a cyclical or special audit, that discipline may be required, the responsible deputy superintendent will investigate. He will prepare a report of her or his findings and make recommendations respecting an appropriate disciplinary measure. The report and recommendations are forwarded to the superintendent and to the trustee. Before the superintendent exercises the disciplinary power, the deputy superintendent will normally discuss the report and recommendations with the trustee in an effort to reach an agreed resolution of the discipline issue.

If the negotiated settlement procedure fails, the matter reverts to the superintendent for decision. However, the superintendent cannot exercise the discipline power without first giving the trustee an opportunity to be heard. This of course means a full open hearing in which the trustee has the right to be heard, the right to call his own evidence, and to contest the evidence against him.

In current practice, a hearing by the superintendent would usually be conducted by an independent neutral third party—again in the current practice, usually a retired member of the judiciary—to whom the superintendent delegates his disciplinary powers under the authority of the statute. This delegation includes the power to impose whatever disciplinary measures are required, including the suspension or revocation of licence. It should be noted, however, that it is the superintendent who is formally vested by statute with the power to decide to investigate, commence disciplinary proceedings and impose disciplinary measures.

It goes without saying that disciplinary decisions must be based on the evidence before the superintendent or his delegate and that discipline decisions, being decisions of a federal board, commission or other tribunal, are subject to judicial review in the Federal Court.

This role of the superintendent as licensor, trainer, standard setter, investigator and disciplinarian would probably be anathema in the United States. On the other hand, a disciplinary process involving a hearing would not be regarded as standard in Europe. Thus once again we have a uniquely Canadian solution that is effective and flexible and not too cumbersome or costly.

Conclusion: staying the course

These four representative examples demonstrate our achievement in attaining this sort of balance between procedural fairness and efficient operation in a wide range of regulatory areas. We have studied precedents in other countries and evolved a unique Canadian regulatory and/or legal product that is both efficient and fair. Our own concept of due process has evolved, relying on our common law connections to natural justice. We have superimposed our regime of substantive and procedural fairness on regulatory structures that are, in some cases, borrowed directly from our American neighbours. It was the United States that created the independent regulatory tribunal which we slowly adopted, along with open, transparent regulatory process. We have, however, tried, and for the most part successfully I trust, to avoid an overemphasis on cumbersome and costly regulatory process and the rigour of technical compliance with it, as well as the general tendency of litigiousness, all of which gets in the way of efficient, fair, and user-friendly regulation. At the same time, we retained, to the greatest extent possible, the flexibility and discretion that is characteristic of European regulatory and administrative models without picking up their lack of transparency and over-deference to state authority. It is my view that we have struck a pretty good balance.

The system is not perfect, however. Its evolution has not stopped, nor should it, and there are several areas that can be improved. For example, many observers have suggested that the

Canadian regime dealing with import and export permits could be tightened up somewhat, to reduce ministerial discretion in the issuance of permits. They suggest the government should establish more statutory or regulatory criteria for the awarding of permits, or adopt an auction procedure for their allocation, or, as a further alternative, establish a review procedure of the decision to award a permit.

In the view of many critics, there is also lots of work to be done to eliminate undue and unnecessary divisions of responsibility within the Canadian system. For example, it has been observed that the responsibility for adjudicating disputes on the classification, valuation or duties payable for imported goods rests with the CITT, while the authority to determine the taxability or the amount of tax payable on such goods rests with the Tax Court of Canada.

It also sometimes seems that every single tribunal at the federal level in Canada has its own procedure. Tribunals are also differently constituted, have different terms of appointment, and different lengths of tenure. There is little doubt that a lot of efficiencies could be gained through standardization, so it would be very useful to have a comprehensive act covering the makeup of tribunals and their procedures that would apply across the board unless some special regime were set up in the legislation pertaining to a particular tribunal. That is not by any means a radical idea. The United States has had such legislation for a long time, as has Ontario, and it seems to work.

In conclusion, Canadians can be justifiably proud of our achievements in building a regulatory system that is both efficient and fair by borrowing precedents from other jurisdictions and adapting them to fit our needs as we think necessary. The proper course for the future, therefore, is to continue to improve our system without radically changing it. We are on the right course, and should stay on it.

An Environmental Right to Sue

MARK MATTSON

In 1994, the federal government initiated consultation on the proposed amendments to the Canadian Environmental Protection Act (CEPA) by setting up the House of Commons Standing Committee on Environment and Sustainable Development. The standing committee reported back to the government in 1995 in a document entitled *It's about Our Health!* One of the many recommendations from that report proposed a CEPA amendment to expand the citizen's right to sue. Unfortunately, while the proposed amendment is directed toward improving enforcement of Canadian environmental laws, it falls short of achieving meaningful progress.

Proposed amendment

The federal government proposes to broaden the right of citizens to sue by removing the current provision that limits standing to parties who suffered loss or damage as a result of a violation of the Canadian Environmental Protection Act (CEPA). The proposed amendment may enable a citizen to initiate a civil action against a party who has violated CEPA where the violation resulted in significant harm to the environment. The civil action is subject to the condition that the citizen makes an application for a government investigation under section 108 of CEPA, and, subsequently, a court determines that the minister took an unreasonable amount of time in responding or that the minister's response was unreasonable. While the government has still not finalized a position on the remedies that will be available to the plaintiff, it is studying the safeguards, rights, and remedies in the current Ontario Environmental Bill of Rights as potential provisions in CEPA and has decided against a provision to allow plaintiffs to receive a portion of the fine or damage awards.

The need for amendment

As noted in the introduction of the Canadian Environmental Protection Act "Enforcement and Compliance Policy," a benchmark for good legislation is that it can be effectively enforced. Enforcement must be fair, nationally consistent, and predictable. Also, those who administer legislation and those who comply with it need to understand how enforcement will be carried out. CEPA falls well short of this benchmark on enforcement.

Currently, the federal government employs only 7 full-time environmental investigators. By comparison, Ontario's investigative and enforcement branch has approximately 60 full-time investigators. Federal investigators initiated only three prosecutions under CEPA from April 1993 to March 1994. Most investigations are dropped due to a lack of time and resources. The standing committee on Environment and Sustainable Development found the record of Environment Canada in enforcing its laws to be disappointing and uneven. It noted that it is highly questionable whether good environmental citizens are being treated fairly.

The lack of federal resources devoted to enforcing environmental laws has resulted in an uneven approach to regulation and investigations. Accordingly, this has eroded the faith of business and public interests groups in the ability of government to enforce consistent environmental standards in Canada.

In light of the failure of the federal government to enforce CEPA effectively, the proposed amendment to CEPA that provides an opportunity for citizens to force the federal government to enforce the law is well intentioned.

Flaws

(1) Although the need to create a right to sue is a direct result of the current lack of enforcement of federal environmental laws, the amendment is drafted so as to further exacerbate the burden on federal investigators and create an even more *ad hoc* basis for enforcement of CEPA provisions.

The requirements that parties file a complaint under section 108 of CEPA, and that a court determine that the minister took an unreasonable time in responding or that the response was unreasonable, will place unnecessary additional burdens on federal investigators. This will make an already bad situation worse. Investigators will be forced to follow up on all public complaints and may be forced to defend any lack of action in court. This will pit the public against federal investigators and will consume investigators' time responding to public complaints.

The benchmark for good legislation—that it must be effectively enforced in a fair, nationally consistent, and predictable manner and that those who administer legislation and those who comply with it need to understand how enforcement will be carried out—will not be achieved through the proposed amendment.

(2) The remedies available to citizens initiating a civil suit have still not been drafted. The standing committee recommended that the court be empowered to order an injunction against the defendants or order the defendant to take remedial action, order the parties to negotiate a restoration plan, order the defendant to pay damages into the special environmental fund to be established under CEPA, and order partial or full recovery of the plaintiffs costs. These remedies are patterned after the remedies in the Ontario Environmental Bill of Rights.

The government also rejected the notion that a civil suit be a means to seek redress for damages arising from activities that are authorized under the CEPA because, it argued, a common law right to bring suits to seek damages already exists.

Obviously, the remedies available under the civil right are essential to the overall effectiveness of the amendment. It is unfortunate that the government has left this crucial issue unresolved. The decision to rule out a remedy that addresses damages arising from activities authorized under the CEPA is unfortunate. The government's reliance on the common law right for damages fails to address the plaintiff's difficult task in convincing a court that a defendant who is abiding by CEPA should pay damages.

(3) The standing committee recommended that the traditional rules of tort liability be amended with respect to civil suits brought under CEPA. The recommendation is that the federal government be encouraged to provide in CEPA a civil remedy for the creation of environmental risk, where measure of damages would be proportional to the increased risk caused by the defendant, and in which, once a plaintiff had presented a *prima facie* case demonstrating that the defendant had caused the environmental risk complained of, the onus would be placed on the defendant to disprove causation of injury to the plaintiff. Currently, the plaintiff must prove on the balance of probabilities that the defendant caused the environmental harm. The government is still reviewing these proposals.

The suggestions from the standing committee stem from the difficult nature of proving that toxic substances caused the specified harm in the complaint. While it can be shown that the toxic substances have contributed to the environmental harm, it is difficult to prove that it caused some specific forms of harm such as health impacts. The government must respond to this very important issue.

(4) The standing committee recommended to government that in addition to the right to sue, the amendments to CEPA include strengthening the ability of the public to prosecute polluters. Currently, a citizen who initiates a private prosecution cannot remain a party to the prosecution if the attorney general assumes control of the case.

The government rejected the standing committee recommendation. It responded that the current law already allows for private prosecutions and that the Criminal Code of Canada allows the attorney general to assume control of the prosecution or stay it. The government rejected the notion of allowing citizens to remain parties to the action if the attorney general assumes control of the case as it would fetter the discretion of the attorney general. A recent example of an attorney general assuming control of a private prosecution and staying the proceeding is currently under appeal in British Columbia. That case involves a private prosecution initiated by Sierra Legal Defence Fund against the Greater Vancouver Regional District for sewage overflows.

(5) The government rejected a fine-splitting provision that would encourage public participation in enforcing CEPA through civil suits and private prosecutions. The suggestion to provide the plaintiff or prosecutor with half the fine awarded by the court as an incentive to protect community resources was also rejected by the standing committee. A precedent for the fine-splitting provision is found in the federal Fisheries Act which justifies the penalty as a method to encourage public participation in the protection of community interests.

The stated reason for rejecting fine splitting was that citizens should not be motivated by the prospect of receiving a share of the monetary penalty but should be motivated by simply the protection of the environment. Unfortunately, the standing committee and the government are wrong in believing that a fine-splitting provision would change the motivation of the group carrying out the prosecution. The standing committee and the government are wrong in rejecting the fine-splitting provisions due to preconceived notions about other parties' motivations. This sort of moral judgement is misdirected and fails to recognize the enormous resources needed to initiate a law suit or that prosecutions will not always result in fines or cost awards sufficient to compensate for expenses incurred. A fine-splitting provision would provide a small incentive to public interest groups to offset the significant financial burdens of initiating civil suits and private prosecutions that protect community interests.

Conclusions

The government proposes to amend CEPA in order to expand the right to initiate a civil suit. It does this by expanding the standing provisions. Further, the government has promised to continue to study changes to the remedies available in CEPA in order to provide safeguards, rights, and remedies such as those in the Ontario Environmental Bill of Rights.

The proposed amendment to broaden the right of the public to have access to the courts in order to enforce environmental laws fails to make all the significant changes required to make the amendment effective. This failure stems from the government's inability to recognize itself as the major impediment to the enforcement of CEPA. The federal government is the problem. It is government intervention that stands in the way of a public right to protect community resources. Specifically, the government rejected amendments of CEPA that would have granted the public an independent right to enforce CEPA provisions through civil suits and private prosecutions. All civil suits and prosecutions arising out of CEPA remain subject to government control, and in the case of prosecutions, can be prevented from continuing. The government should not prevent the public from pursuing its own remedies.

In the final analysis, the government holds out the promise that the new amendments to CEPA will provide opportunities for zealous and conscientious interests to prod government action and seek legal solutions to remedy environmental harm to community interests. Unfortunately, the amendments may do nothing more than further the administrative burden on federal investigators, who already have too few resources to enforce the Canadian Environmental Protection Act.

Will We Be Back in Five Years?

The Report of the Canadian Bar Association Task Force

Seymour B. Trachimovsky

The Canadian Bar Association Task Force

The Canadian Bar Association (CBA) recently released the Task Force Report in respect of the Systems of Civil Justice (the Report). The Task Force, of which I was a member, was charged to inquire into the state of the civil justice system on a national basis and to develop strategies and mechanisms to facilitate modernization of the justice system so that it is better able to meet current and future needs of Canadians. Our Task Force made some 50 recommendations in this regard and I am pleased to say that the Report has generally been greeted with applause from all corners of the legal profession: judges, academics, practitioners, and legal journalists. This is gratifying and at least mildly surprising since the report in some respects calls for fundamental change in the way in which legal services are delivered today by the profession. Change is not typically greeted

Notes will be found on page 144.

with an ovation from the very people who are being called upon to make the transformation.

The ideal pursued by the Task Force, as expressed in our mandate, was a justice system that is "more efficient, accessible, accountable, fair, and able to deliver timely results in a cost effective manner." Our focus, in brief, was cost and delay. Although it is often assumed that dealing with the one is equivalent to dealing with the other, that is not invariably the case and, indeed, it is my suspicion that the implementation of our recommendations will meliorate the latter more readily than it will the former. Some personal reflections on the Report's recommendations and on some of the commentary it has precipitated will clarify the reasons for that suspicion.

Recommendations of the task force

Procedural costs

The Report calls for the introduction of a variety of procedural measures intended to encourage settlement of lawsuits prior to trial, measures which it recommended be made mandatory as a condition for proceeding to a full trial. Some skeptics have argued that these procedures will impose additional costs on litigants without any return. That is a valid criticism in that for a minority of cases that cannot be settled through the additional mechanisms we recommend, the cost of litigation may in fact increase. But overall the cost of litigation should be reduced because most cases, it is hoped, will be settled sooner. Our emphasis has been on *settlement*, on providing the parties with as much opportunity and incentive as possible to resolve their differences privately before a dispute gets out of control. Indeed, if our recommendations are implemented, the pursuit of settlement will become an obligation for the parties and for their counsel. Whether an opportunity or an obligation, the failure to settle at an early stage may give rise to additional costs. But even here it will depend upon which of the recommended tracks is selected to resolve the dispute.

As a consequence, the Report puts a premium on *reasonable conduct*. Parties who act reasonably will benefit from the new approaches. Regrettably, every lawyer has seen unreasonable conduct on both sides of the table—from his own client or his opponent's client. I was impressed, in the course of our discussions and deliberations, that as lawyers we were prepared to accept exclusive responsibility for the many flaws of the system. While that is an honourable gesture, it is not entirely correct for as often as not it is in fact the obdurate client who causes litigation to be protracted and wasteful. Under certain kinds of legal rules, as other contributors to this volume have noted, there can be a considerable incentive for a party to act unreasonably and I believe that this problem is at the core of the explosive growth of litigation, a matter to which I will return later in this paper.

The pursuit of perfect justice

A comment that came up repeatedly in Task Force consultations (delivered with considerable passion in some cases I might add) is that the reforms we were likely to recommend—Alternative Dispute Resolution (ADR), expedited procedures, and so on—would somehow impair the quality of justice delivered by the system. To the fundamentalists who make this point, a pristine legal process is an overarching goal. Everything must be subordinated to the ultimate delivery of a 100 percent immaculate judicial decision. Related to this is a second argument against private arbitration emanating from some quarters, specifically that private decisions do not enter the public domain of jurisprudence to become part of the legal canon.

The second argument is not in my view justified. It depends for its integrity on the existence on some kind of public right—beyond merely a public interest—in the resolution of private disputes and that right clearly does not exist. There are numerous arguments against this position ranging from the fiscal to the philosophical but space precludes a discussion of them.

Returning to the first point, I think it is trite to say that perfect justice is an unattainable goal. So what? say fundamentalists, it is the highest ideal of our legal system and one, therefore, that we must pursue unrelentingly even if we can never reach it. But, as the expression goes, "the best is the enemy of the good." The zealous pursuit of some ideal on theoretical grounds can easily become counter-productive. Thus, it is the myriad procedural safeguards we have built into our system that are the playing field of obstructionist parties and their counsel and so actually move us away from perfect justice. The more we have constructed procedures to achieve that goal, the more it has receded.

An important though far from everyday example is that every lawyer is aware of a number of issues in his or her practice area that are in need of authoritative resolution, preferably by our Supreme Court. Most of these issues will never appear on the docket of the Supreme Court because it is overwhelmed with a great number of appeals as of right in certain criminal cases, appeals that have the effect of preempting civil matters. Thus overzealousness with respect to criminal procedure so obstructs civil procedure that on balance we have less rather than more justice. This is an issue touched upon by our Task Force only in passing but I think is one that will merit a great deal of future scrutiny. There is almost nothing, save perhaps constitutional references at the request of Government, that should go as of right to our Supreme Court with its limited docket of 100 to 125 appeals heard annually.

Change in legal culture

Another major recommendation of the Task Force Report is, in effect, a call for a change in legal culture, from an adversarial profession eager to do battle in the court room to one that views the court room as a last resort. Remedies requiring cultural change are generally dubious because in many cases they are empty and impracticable, even a sign that things are probably hopeless. Further, given that the particular subject is litigation, it must be remembered that disputes are inherently adversarial and always will be. Fortunately, there is nevertheless some reason to be optimistic—the image of the "Rambo lawyer", at least in Canada, is exaggerated. Most of the litigation bar is already disposed to achieve out of court settlement and it is often the client, not his counsel, who is implacable.

Such optimism, however, must be tempered by developments outside the jurisdiction of the Task Force moving the profession in precisely the opposite direction, particularly the probability of expanded private rights of action under a variety of statutes.

Judicial oversight of case management

Implementation of the Task Force recommendations would invest the Courts with considerably more authority to influence the course of an action than has traditionally been the case. This could be a parlous course but it is unavoidable given the slow pace at which cases move and the consequent enormous backlog.

The basic problem is that there is too little accountability in our system for the pace at which an action proceeds through the court. The consequences are scandalous. There are few features of the American civil justice system that most sensible people would want transferred to Canada, (*e.g.*, limited cost indemnification, punitive damages, extensive discoveries, widespread jury trials, elected judiciary); however, if nothing else, Americans move a case through the system much more rapidly than we are able to and it starts with a strong case management system with close judicial oversight. Because this gives judges further dramatic powers to influence the outcome of cases, an important point is that the quality of the judiciary, ever a crucial variable, will become more so and the selection process a more critical matter if such a system is implemented.

Resources

Last but hardly least among the Task Force recommendations are those made concerning the matter of resources. A number of judges we spoke to limned a bleak portrait of the modern court house suffocating under the weight of a century-old infrastructure. There is probably ample truth in that picture. And it is also true that some capital expenditures today would reap a substantial social return. The reality, however, is that the system of justice must compete for public funds against innumerable other socially necessary, desirable, or at least popular activities such as health care, education, and welfare, to name but a few. The trauma recently confronting these programs is front and centre on the 6 o'clock news every day.

It is also important to note the apparently obvious but frequently overlooked point that the enactment of new statutes on a regular basis to appease one or another segment of the electorate or the promulgation of various regulations further increases the burden on the courts. You cannot pass laws without exerting pressure of some sort on the justice system, and legislatures ought to devote much more attention than they do to ensuring that sufficient additional resources are provided to cope with the additional stress on the courts.

However, before any specific recommendation can be made for the allocation of additional resources to the system of justice or, indeed, to law enforcement generally, it is time to take stock of present resources and to assess whether they are being used wisely. In the absence of data, unfortunately, we are left to speculate, so the first thing we need here is more and better data.

Conclusion: the task force next time

One much larger phenomenon, beyond the scope of the Task Force, also requires serious consideration. I believe firmly, all things being equal, that the road map we have drawn in the Report will lead, for reasonable parties, to a better justice system—more effective and more efficient. The caveat, of course, is the "all things being equal" and here there is less reason to be optimistic. At the CBA Conference last August, one concerned observer queried whether we would be back in five years to try again. My view is that we are indeed likely to be back.

A tidal wave of arcane law

It is one thing to muzzle the pit-bull litigator, and our recommendations would help achieve that. But it is quite another to stand in the way of a tidal wave of new law and regulation and a concurrent trend in favour of actively encouraging litigation as an instrument of social change. Here I would like to cite Professor Richard A. Epstein of the University of Chicago in his recent brilliant and ambitious work, *Simple Rules for a Complex World*:

> Although there are isolated instances of the contraction of legal claims, the general trend is quite in the opposite direction: more law. Our aspirations for what a legal system can do to improve social circumstances is simply too high. We try to solve more and more problems through legal intervention, and fewer through voluntary accommodation and informal practices. A kind of Gresham's law has set in, for the increased dependence on lawyers and legal proceedings renders the informal modes of doing business less effective. Any individual case may well present appealing reasons for some new statutory intervention (the adoption of family leave legislation is one recent battle), but the combined or cumulative effect of countless legal innovations tends to be ignored in the ceaseless quest to adopt any single innovation. What appears noble in the individual case turns out to be dubious in the aggregate. By degrees, therefore, our extensive level of social ambition leads us to a very complex set of legal rules, one which only lawyers can understand and navigate, and then at very stiff fees. The virtue of simplicity, around which this book is organized, is never deprecated, but it does suffer from insufficient respect and appreciation.

> By degrees we find that private and public actors all must resort to the use of lawyers, or to administrators steeped in the law, in order to solve their particular problems.[1]

In defining complexity, Professor Epstein refers to an analysis of the subject by Peter Schuck, who has organized the field by reference to four distinct variables that he regards as the markers of a complex set of legal rules: density, technicality, differentiation, and indeterminacy or uncertainty. Dense legal rules are numerous and cover in minute detail all aspects of a given transaction: who may participate, what forms must be used, what terms are allowed, what approvals must be obtained. Technical rules are those that require a certain level of expertise to understand and apply. Differentiation refers to the number of different sources of law that could be brought to bear in a given situation, often in an overlapping or inconsistent fashion. Schuck's last test stresses the level of uncertainty that is generated in the effort to apply a given rule. In essence, a question that necessarily has a yes or no answer—is the defendant liable to the plaintiff—is not governed by some simple on/off switch but by a massive, costly, and uncertain inquiry.

Professor Epstein adds his own crucial addition—pervasiveness—to Schuck's analysis:

> For my purposes at least, a complex rule is one that, in addition to meeting Schuck's criteria, has *pervasive application* across routine social activities, and is not directed solely to the dangerous activities of people who live at the margins of society. Legal complexity is not merely a simple measure of the inherent or formal properties of legal rules. It is also a function of how deeply they cut into the fabric of ordinary life.[2]

I was struck, not long after reading the above, by the following discussion of trademark law in a recent issue of the American publication, *Of Counsel*:

> It's quite a challenge to advise clients in such a murky legal climate. Oftentimes, there's just no telling what an outcome will be, (trade mark lawyer) Bridges says. "My client looks to me to articulate risks as clearly as possible. However, trademark law is totally subjective. I often tell clients that I am absolutely sure that the outcome is uncertain" . . .

> Because trademark law is not cut-and-dry, the potential for litigation is high, (trade mark lawyer) Bridges says. "Most of my clients wind up in litigation [in] areas where the law is unclear. The cases that get fought, and get fought with a lot of money, are [the ones] where both parties think [it] can go their way."

Virtually every legal practitioner will recognize that what Mr. Bridges has to say about trademark law can apply just as well to his or her field of expertise. Mark these words: "the potential for litigation is high." Superimpose on this the philosophy that argues for more opportunities for public litigation, prosecution and so on in more and more areas, and there is less reason for optimism than the more mundane aspects of the Task Force report would suggest.

If we create more law, more uncertainty, more opportunity and incentive to litigate, then we will certainly see you again in 5 years for another Task Force Report.

Notes

1 Richard A. Epstein, *Simple Rules for a Complex World*, Cambridge, MA: Harvard University Press, 1995: 14.

2 *Ibid.*: 29.

The State of Canadian Judicial Statistics

Trends in Canadian Civil Justice

OWEN LIPPERT, STEPHEN EASTON, AND CRAIG YIRUSH

The law provides the principal means of non-market decision-making. Yet we know very little about the law's impact on the Canadian economy and on its constituent markets. Other contributors to this volume have discussed individual cases, possible or actual rule changes and their likely impact, and suggested administrative regimes to improve the efficiency of justice. It is important that we evaluate these systematically in light of what is already happening. But this is very difficult to do at present. We lack even basic measurements of public and private spending on legal services. We do not know how many individuals and companies are engaged in legal processes. Without such fundamental statistical building blocks, it is difficult to measure and to understand the law's efficiency, distribution, and equity effects. The study of law and economics in Canada, to date, has not had an empirical check. The consequences may be that:

- economic growth, efficiency and fairness have suffered

Notes will be found on pages 174–77.

- current policies and approaches continue unchecked to perpetuate inefficiencies
- proposed reforms will either not make a difference or actually cause economic harm.

The first requirement for answering these questions is more and better information. Our purpose here is to the theory of measuring legal expenditures and outputs and to give examples of actual measurements, both to show what it is already possible to determine and also to show what it might be possible to determine if better and more systematic information were available. The results are organized according to a basic identity equation of legal spending and outputs. Three major data sets are used:

(1) an innovative *Public Accounts*-based measurement of public sector justice spending;

(2) court case data from provincial courts; and

(3) a survey of the members of the Canadian Corporate Counsel Association.

We reach a number of tentative conclusions in our work, but the one that stands out is that we desperately need more and better information on this subject.

The identity equation

One can, in principle, fairly easily characterize the costs of the Canadian civil justice system. You first calculate what consumers, governments, and business spend on civil justice, and then relate that to what the providers of legal services, private law firms, courts, regulatory authorities, and government justice personnel, receive to support their activities. (Obviously some of this spending goes to support legal activities concerning criminal law that cannot yet be broken out fully). Alternatively, you can relate costs to what is spent on outputs such as actions and trials. This allows for some simple comparative analysis of efficiency within the legal system. One jurisdiction can be compared to another on the basis of cost per action or cost per trial.

The reason for using an identity equation is that it allows for a broad understanding of these relationships even when the statistical evidence is incomplete. It is simply a way to organize the data.

The basic identity that relates expenditures and receipts is:

$$C + G + B = L + J + R,$$

where the *expenditure* side: C = consumer spending, G = government spending, and B = business (or producer) spending. The receipts of these expenditures are to be found in: L = private law firm income and costs (including in-house counsel), J = court salaries plus public sector justice personnel salaries and costs, and R = regulatory salaries and costs. These expenditures and receipts change over time and must be related to one another.

The basic formula to explain how and to what degree they change is:

$$\theta_C\hat{C} + \theta_G\hat{G} + \theta_B\hat{B} = \theta_L\hat{L} + \theta_J\hat{J} + \theta_R\hat{R}$$

The hat (^) over a variable represents the percentage rate of change of that variable. The thetas (θ) are the shares that each component (identified in the subscript) comprises in the total. For example, θ_C refers to the share of total expenditures on civil justice spent by consumers. The θ's add up to unity on each side of the equation since the total amount spent is allocated among the categories on the left-hand side, and the total amount received is allocated among the categories on the right-hand side.

The use of the above accounting identity to categorize expenditures and receipts of the civil justice system is difficult to implement in practice. We do not have a national accounting system that permits a natural decomposition into reasonable categories. One important contribution of our research has been to build a set of figures for each side of the identity, but there are sufficient gaps among the classifications; as such, we feel more comfortable looking at each side individually. That is, we first examine the spending that takes place on civil legal services and then turn to the recipients of those expenditures.

The components of civil legal spending

The components of civil legal spending have been developed from several sources and are not available on a consistent basis every year. We have chosen four years, 1973/74, 1980/81, 1987/88 and 1993/94 as our benchmark years, ones for which Dr. Paul Reed of Statistics Canada has provided a far more extensive breakdown of the justice system's accounts than is available elsewhere.

The *Overview* part of this section gives a summary of the entire twenty year period. The second section breaks the totals into smaller subperiods. Although the general trends described in the overview are both interesting and important, the subperiods highlight the fluctuations that have occurred in the growth rates.

Overview

In table 1, we report an overview of the growth of the components of justice spending. In this table the first row of the first column gives the average annual real growth in spending. That is, the inflation adjusted increase in civil justice spending from all sources is 2.3 percent per year between 1973/74 and 1993/94. This growth rate reflects real expenditures in the sense that it is not due simply to an increase in the level of general consumer prices, but reflects increases in expenditures once the growth in the general level of prices has been taken into account.

Table 1 Average annual real growth of civil legal spending by major customer groups from 1973/74 to 1993/94

All groups	Consumers	Government	Business
2.3%	3.9%	2.9%	0.9%
Percent contributed to total growth			
[100%]*	19.2%	66.9%	13.4%

* Rounding error means the row totals may not add up exactly.

Reading across the first row, we see that the components of spending are all on the rise over this period. Reading from the second column, the average annual growth rate of consumer spending is 3.9 percent per year.[1] Thus consumers on average over this period have increased their spending more than business and government. In the third column, we can see that the rate of government spending on civil legal services has increased by 2.9 percent per year on average, and in the final column we observe that business expenditures have increased by 0.9 percent per year on average.

Because the different components of expenditures are of different sizes, the effect of the growth rates of the individual components on the overall rate of growth is substantial. These relationships are described in row 2 of the table. Of the average

2.3 percent per year real annual growth, 19.2 percent of that growth is attributable to increases in the growth of consumer spending. Government spending has increased at a rate of 2.9 percent per year annual real growth, and as over half of all spending on civil legal services is by governments, it accounts for 66.9 percent of the overall 2.3 percent per year growth in total spending on legal services. At 0.9 percent per year, business spending on civil legal services grew at a rate well below that of the other two sectors of the market for civil legal services. Despite its size (35 percent of all expenditures on civil legal services), its contribution to the overall growth rate was only 13.4 percent of the 2.3 percent increase in average annual expenditures.

These increases make up all of the increase in spending on civil legal services, which have grown in dollar value from $1.9 billion in 1973 to just over $11 billion by 1993. The greatest contributor to the growth rate of spending is government, followed by consumer spending and then spending by business.

Since whatever is spent on legal services must be received by the providers of legal services, table 2 describes the growth of the receipts side of the identity equation.[2] The first row of table 2 reports the rates of growth by recipient category. Reading across the first row tells us that law firm receipts grew on average at 2.1 percent per year, which is less quickly than overall receipts and, of course, spending. Regulatory providers had revenues that grew at 2.5 percent per year and also grew less rapidly than the average. The growth in receipts on court and justice personnel and costs rose much more quickly on average during this period than either of the other two categories at an average rate of 5.2 percent per year. All percentages are average annual real (inflation adjusted) growth rates.

Table 2 Average annual real growth of civil legal receipts by major recipient groups from 1973/74 to 1993/94

All receipts	Private law firms	Court, justice personnel etc.	Regulatory salaries and costs
2.6%	2.1%	5.2%	2.5%
Percent contributed to total growth			
[100%]*	35.4%	19.6%	45.8%

* Rounding error means the row totals may not add up exactly.

The contribution that each of these categories makes to overall growth depends both on the rate of increase of the category itself and the size of the category in the total of all receipts. In this case, the contribution that each category makes to the total is shown in the second row of the table. In the case of law firm receipts, which amount to about 43 percent of total income received (on average during the 20 years), the contribution to the total growth of all receipts is 35.4 percent. That is, the growth rate of 2.1 percent accounts for 35 percent of all receipt growth. Similarly, the 2.5 percent growth in regulatory agency costs and salaries, because it amounts to 47 percent of all salaries and costs, accounts for almost 46 percent of all growth in receipts from civil justice expenditures. Although court and justice personnel and costs amount to only 10 percent of all spending on civil justice, the average increase in spending for court and justice personnel and costs means that the relatively high 5.2 percent per year annual growth accounts for nearly 20 percent (19.6 percent) of all the increases in spending on civil justice.

The years between 1973/74 and 1993/94: a more detailed view of various subperiods

It would be a mistake to take these annual average real growth rates of expenditure categories as the best or most appropriate representation of the growth rates of expenditures on civil legal justice. Although it would be desirable to have annual estimates of each of these categories, the data currently available do not permit us to do so. Instead, we have particular dates for which the accounts can be fleshed out. These are based on the years chosen by Dr. Reed of Statistics Canada, who has conducted a special analysis at the request of The Fraser Institute and the Canadian Bar Association. The period to period average growth rates are presented in tables 3 and 4.

In table 3 we can see, by looking at column 1, that the average increases in spending rose most rapidly in the mid-1980s, with the slowest rate of growth in the late 1980s and early 1990s. Of all the components, consumer spending rose throughout our 20-year period, and was growing more rapidly than any other component of spending by the final seven years. Business spending on legal services appears to have fallen in all but one of the three periods examined. Government spending on legal matters has shown constant growth over our twenty year period, with a particularly high annual growth rate from 1974 to 1980.

Table 3 Detailed average annual real growth of civil legal spending by major customer group from 1973/74 to 1993/94

Years	All groups	Consumers	Business	Government
1974–1980	2.6%	1.6%	-0.1%	5.1%
1980–1987	4.8%	4.5%	7.0%	2.0%
1987–1994	0.1%	6.0%	-3.4%	1.5%

Looking at table 4, we can see that the recipients of expenditures have growth patterns that display variability that is as great as on the expenditure side of the ledger. Law-firm income grew in the mid-1980s, but growth was stagnant or in slight decline both before and after. The costs of justice and court personnel and associated costs was the fastest growing category in all but the mid-1980s, while regulatory costs have been increasing at a more or less constant rate since 1980. This average annual increase in regulatory costs is particularly interesting as it is almost half of all justice system costs.

Table 4 Detailed average annual real growth of civil legal receipts by major recipient groups from 1973/74 to 1993/94

Years	Private Law Firms	Court, justice personnel etc.*	Regulatory salaries and costs
1974–1980	0.0%	7.2%	4.7%
1980–1987	6.3%	5.6%	1.2%
1987–1994	–0.3%	2.4%	1.3%

* These costs include salaries and benefits, court services, transportation and a pro rata share of other fixed costs drawn from the public accounts

In Canada, on average over the last 20 years, 54 percent of civil legal expenditures have been spent by the government, 35 percent by the business community, and 11 percent by the consumer. Of course the "consumer" and the taxpayer pay all the bills in an ultimate sense, but we divide expenditures into these categories as we expect decisions about spending on civil justice to be determined differently by each group. These expenditures are heavily weighted toward government, and, secondarily, business. Receiving these expenditures are regulatory authorities, commissions, tribunals, and the like at 47 percent of all revenues, private law firms at 43 percent, and the court and justice system at 10 percent. Over the 20 years, the fastest growth has taken place in the use of the court and justice system.

One way to understand the behaviour of the people who are making the expenditures or receiving the income is to disaggregate the expenditure and receipt components of the identity formula. We illustrate this below.

Consumer legal spending and its changes

Legal-services spending by consumers is the fastest growing of all the components of expenditures. Within the two classes of spending identified by Statistics Canada, consumer spending (not including accommodation) is the fastest growing. Legal services spending by consumers has two components: consumer legal spending for "accommodation," S.C. 2702 in the Family Expenditure Survey (FES), and consumer legal spending "not elsewhere specified," S.C. 3603 in the Family Expenditure Survey. The latter includes automobile injury claims, divorce proceedings, and other personal legal actions. It is worth noting that Statistics Canada does not gather data on S.C. 3603 categories except as an aggregate.

Table 5 summarizes a decade of consumer spending, excluding accommodation.[3] The first two rows of the first column of the table reports the level of non-accommodation legal spending by the average family for 1982 and 1992. The third row reports the average annual rate of growth of that spending. As a comparison, the second column reports the average per capita level of gross domestic product, the GDP. This is a useful summary measure of the richness of the country. As is apparent from the different growth rates, while per capita income (GDP) rose on average about one and one-half percent per year during the decade from 1982 to 1992, the growth in legal services spending (other than for accommodation) rose at nearly 5 percent per year. In 1993/94 dollars, total consumer spending for civil legal services amount to some $1.6 billion.

As our economy is growing, consumers are becoming increasingly litigious as measured by the average amount consumers are willing to spend on legal services in each family.[4]

Table 5 **Consumer spending on legal services (excluding accommodation) 1982 to1992, compared to GDP**

Year	Per family*	Per-capita GDP*
1982	$66.00	$16,953.00
1992	$108.00	$19,622.00
Average annual growth rates		
	4.9%	1.5%

Source: Statistics Canada, *Family Expenditure in Canada* Cat. no. 62-555, 1982 and 1992 versions

* Real (inflation adjusted) 1994 dollars

Government legal spending and its changes

Another way to see who is spending on what services is to look at the government accounts more closely. In this case we look at spending on the courts and regulatory agencies by level of government. Table 6 draws directly from Dr. Paul Reed's *Public Accounts*-based analysis of public sector spending on justice services. It covers both federal, provincial, and municipal spending. He has sampled the years 1973/74, 1980/81, 1987/88, and 1993/94. This will be the first time in Canada that such an extensive and accurate picture of public sector justice spending has been presented. In this context we highlight the changes in spending as a function of the level of government between 1973/74 and 1993/94. In the first two columns we identify the growth rate in the real (inflation adjusted) resources received by the courts and regulatory agencies. For comparison, we add to this the amounts given to other aspects of the justice system in columns three and four, as well as a total of the growth in all of these components of expenditures on the administration of justice in column 5. Government spending in 1993/94 amounted to $6.1 billion on civil justice.

As is apparent from the table, the growth in federal spending on the courts is faster than that of the provinces. By the same token, provincial spending growth is greater than federal on regulatory agencies. Law enforcement expenditure growth is less than the growth of expenditures on the courts at both the federal and provincial level, while the same is true for spending on corrections at the provincial level.

Table 6 Real average annual rate of growth of consolidated government spending on the administration of justice from 1973/74 to 1993/94

Government	Courts*	Regulatory	Law enforcement	Penal/ Corrective	Average
Provincial/ Municipal	4.4%	4.0%	3.1%	3.9%	3.6%
Federal	7.8%	1.5%	4.4%	4.5%	3.2%
Total	5.2%	2.5%	3.4%	4.2%	3.5%

* These costs include salaries and benefits, court services, transportation and a *pro rata* share of other fixed costs drawn from the public accounts.

Civil legal aid is an additional component of government spending on the civil justice system. Between 1973/74 and 1993/94, legal aid grew at a rate of 8.8 percent per year. Since 1980, spending on civil justice has been outpacing the growth in criminal legal-aid spending. The total amount spent on legal aid in 1993/94 is about $600 million, divided roughly in half between civil and criminal.

Business legal spending

Business legal services spending covers both in-house and contracted out legal services. The calculation of in-house spending uses a percentage derived from the survey of the Canadian Corporate Counsel Association members. From the survey, roughly 28 percent of legal costs of business are in-house. The cost of business spending contracted out is obtained by subtracting from the total fees received by law firms, the amounts spent by consumers and by governments on legal aid (minus staff legal-aid providers) and private counsel.[5] The basic formula is

$$B = (L - A - Z - C) + I = L' + I$$

where L = private law firm income, A = Payments to legal aid providers, Z = government spending on private counsel, I = in-house counsel and support costs, C = consumer spending. The only reason for not exploring changes in this decomposition further is that while we have the breakdown on in-house and contracted out legal spending for one year, the period of our survey, we do not have independent evidence of the time pattern of in-house legal spending. To our knowledge, this breakdown is not fully available for earlier periods.[6]

A basic microeconomic view of the output of the civil legal system

The previous section outlined a way to match what is spent with who receives it. This section goes beyond that to match what is spent with what is produced, the output. It is a way to decompose the services provided by the courts, private counsel, public sector and regulatory authorities. There are four outputs measured:

(1) costs per case and costs per trial

(2) costs per input (the resource mix)

(3) costs of delay

(4) user satisfaction (CCCA survey results)

Caseload and trials

Basic outputs are the cases and trials handled by each element of the legal system. The focus in the presentation will be on the provincial superior trial courts. Only Ontario consistently provides detailed information on caseloads and trials. The statistics from other provinces are considerably less complete.

By matching spending to caseloads and trials, one can create basic efficiency measures of cost and quantity. What is the aggregate cost per trial? What is the aggregate cost per action? On a per-capita basis, which provinces have the most and the least expensive caseloads and trials? With the *Public Accounts*-based justice spending statistics and the caseloads, comparisons can be made over time and across jurisdictions.

We start by modeling the per-action value of expenditure (you could also choose the per-trial value). This measures the intensity of use. The equation is simply C (consumer spending) equals per-action cost times the number of consumer cases: $C = (C/N_C)N_C$, where N refers to the number of actions, cases, or trials as required. This is repeated for each of the left-hand side components of the identity formula, C, G, and B.

One can further decompose the costs into a per-action cost and litigation intent (action filing) rate by dividing the number of cases, N, by the population, P, in each province.

$$\left[\left(\frac{C}{N_C}\right)\left(\frac{N_C}{P}\right)+\left(\frac{G}{N_G}\right)\left(\frac{N_G}{P}\right)+\left(\frac{B}{N_B}\right)\left(\frac{N_B}{P}\right)\right]\times P = C + G + B$$

Although to date it has only been possible to gather sufficient data to permit such a calculation in a couple of provinces, we have been able to obtain information on filing activity from 7 provinces and one territory. These data are presented in table 7. For the few years for which data can be recovered, we note that the rate of civil filings (or whatever comparable category is used in the different provinces), shows a decline over the last 5 years. This decline is not steady, however, and with such a short time period, it is not clear what role business cycles and other national conditions play, as compared to changes in legislation (*e.g.*, the introduction of no-fault automobile insurance), or the variability of specific local conditions. Whatever the source, there is marginally less civil litigation filed now than in 1990 in all of the provinces for which we have data; the decline is most pronounced in Ontario.

Table 7 Provincial superior court civil filings per 1000 of provincial population

Year	BC	AB	SK	MB	ON	PQ	NB*	NF*	NT
1990	22.9	20.8	16.8	13.5	19.6	15.1	9.8	7.0	na
1991	21.5	22.3	16.6	13.4	21.2	17.0	10.2	6.9	22.3
1992	20.9	21.1	15.9	13.5	16.8	16.0	10.4	7.3	15.3
1993	18.9	19.6	15.0	13.6	13.2	14.0	9.7	7.9	15.4
1994	18.7	19.1	14.7	13.3	11.9	na	9.6	7.2	18.0

* Does not include family court

We have obtained some information about the number of trials conducted by the court system in various provinces. For comparative purposes, in table 8 we reproduce the rate of filing in the four provinces for which we have such trial information.[7]

In each province it is clear there is a ratio of 2 to 4 percent of all actions that end in trial. With so few observations, however, it is difficult to see any particular trend, except in Ontario where we observe a fall in the proportion of trials to filings. This is as might be expected with the change in legislation.[8]

From the perspective of system output, there have been marginally fewer civil actions filed during the past five years. Of these actions, roughly the same proportion goes to trial. The others continue to be disposed of in non-trial related ways. It is unfortunate that data are not collected to permit more extensive comparisons across provinces or over a longer period of time.

Table 8 Provincial superior court civil filings and trials in selected provinces

Year	BC	AB	SK	NB	ON
Filings per 1000 of population					
1990	22.9	20.8	16.8	9.8	19.6
1991	21.5	22.3	16.6	10.2	21.2
1992	20.9	21.1	15.9	10.4	16.8
1993	18.9	19.6	15.0	9.7	13.2
1994	18.7	19.1	14.7	9.6	11.9
Percentage of cases filed going to trial.					
1990	na	3.1%	2.5%	na	5.3%
1991	na	2.1%	1.8%	5.5%	4.4%
1992	3.3%	2.7%	2.1%	4.8%	3.1%
1993	3.4%	2.3%	2.5%	4.3%	3.4%
1994	3.3%	2.6%	2.3%	3.5%	3.1%

Costs per input

The right hand side components of the identity formula, *L*, *J*, and *R*, can be decomposed using the same procedure. It can be further broken down into specific inputs such as judges, court personnel, or government lawyers, and, even further, by salary and non-salary costs. By using the "receipt" cost of each input, one can measure provincial variations and changes across time in terms of the input mix used to achieve a given level of output.

Each component is expressed as the sum of the growth rates of its constituent elements. For the courts, you would have the number of salaried recipients, *N*, their average salary, *s*, and the growth of other costs, *O*.

$$\hat{J} = \lambda_{JNW}\,(\hat{N}_J + \hat{s}_J) + \lambda_{JO}\hat{O}_J$$

Depending on how fine-grained you want the analysis, you can keep breaking the expenditures down to the limits of the data provided by the *Public Accounts*. Because the reporting system differs widely amongst provinces, it is difficult to develop a systematic analysis. Given the limits of the court data, we can proceed from here to outlining the per-trial costs.

Cost per trial

To get an idea of the cost to the justice system of running a provincial superior court civil trial, we have completed the following estimate of expenditure per civil trial for Ontario and British Columbia. First, calculate what it costs to run the province's courts per year.[9] Next, separate out the share of this overall cost of running the courts that is attributable to civil cases at the superior trial court level. Since existing data do not account for this figure directly, it is derived by apportioning a share of the overall court operations budget to the superior court, and calculating the share attributable to civil cases. First, we apportion the expenditures between the Provincial Courts and the Superior Courts on the basis of the number of trial court hours in each court. Using this estimate of the province's courts budget devoted to the superior trial court, we then apportion costs between the civil and the criminal sides of the superior court on the basis of the superior trial court hours devoted to each activity. This gives us an estimate of what it costs to run the civil side of the superior trial court. In conjunction with the existing caseload figures on the number of trials, we then derive an average cost per trial.[10] This is done for Ontario and British Columbia in tables 9 and 10 below.

Table 9 Ontario court expenditures in 1993/94

Total, General Division court and judicial support	$263,573,000*
***Civil* share of General Division**	$59,400,000†
General Division civil trial hours in 1993/94	51,031‡
Number of General Division civil trials in 1993/94	4,111**
Average cost per trial	$14, 400††

* Source: *Public Accounts* data provided by Dr. Paul Reed of Statistics Canada.

† This figure includes Section 96 salaries, apportioned between civil and criminal on the basis of the number of General Division trial-court hours devoted to each. It also includes an estimate of the General Division civil share of the *Judicial Services* budget, less the salaries of the provincial Division justices.

‡ Source: Ontario Ministry of the Attorney General, *Civil Justice Review* (1995): 76.

** Source: *Court Statistics Annual Report, 1993/94* (Ontario, Ministry of the Attorney General, 1995).

†† Rounded to the nearest hundred.

A similar calculation is done for Brtish Columbia, again by separating out the share of total judicial and court spending attributable to the civil side of the B.C. Supreme Court, and then arriving at an average cost per trial.

Table 10 British Columbia court expenditures in 1993/94

Total	$125,174,000*
Supreme Court civil	$41,680,000
Supreme Court civil hours in 1993/94	20,463†
Supreme Court trials in 1993/94	2,307‡
Average cost per trial	$18,000**

* Source: British Columbia *Public Accounts*, 1993/94, provided by Dr. Paul Reed of Statistics Canada.

† Source: British Columbia Ministry of the Attorney General, Courts Services Division.

‡ At present, British Columbia's Ministry of the Attorney General does not record the number of Supreme Court trials on a province-wide basis. We have arrived at our figure by taking the number of civil trials held in the Vancouver Registry of the British Columbia Supreme Court, and adjusting this up to a provincial total by using the ratio of provincial civil filings to Vancouver civil filings. The Vancouver civil trials figure was provided by the Law Officer of the Vancouver Supreme Court.

** Rounded to the nearest hundred

These estimates should be expanded and refined, but to do so more data must be available from the courts. The Rand Institute in California, using the vastly better data available from the United States courts, has done a cost calculation for tort cases in three state courts.[11] Rand builds their cost calculations up from microdata on individual case times and costs. To replicate this in Canada would require detailed access to the court records by a team of researchers. We are aware that the Ontario *Civil Justice Review* has plans to do such calculations of the cost per trial for Ontario's Court of Justice (General Division). Unfortunately, the release date of the *Review* has been set back from March until April 1996. We await the results of their work with interest. In the meantime we offer our work as a working estimate for two Canadian jurisdictions, and as a starting point for future discussion.

These estimates for Ontario and British Columbia reflect the costs per trial.[12] As discussed below, there are other breakdowns that are possible conceptually. Costs could be analyzed on a per-filing basis, for example. Our belief, however, is that the cost per trial highlights the essential ingredient that parties want when they come to the courts for dispute resolution. Our calculation reflects the cost to the public of providing the resources needed to resolve these disputes.

Given a more detailed breakdown of the *Public Accounts,* we could break out the cost per trial into its growth components.[13] For example, the total cost per trial is broken up as the total per category. The total cost per trial (TC/T) of our civil legal expenditures in growth terms look like:

$$(\widehat{TC/T}) = \theta_L(\hat{L} - \hat{T}) + \theta_J(\hat{J} - \hat{T}) + \theta_R(\hat{R} - \hat{T})$$

Once again, the *thetas* (θ) are the shares that each component comprises in the total. The hat (^) over a variable represents the percentage rate of change of that variable.

This can be converted to a per-capita breakdown of the costs of the receipts and the particular resource mix used per trial. The equation for judiciary, J, and its salary and related costs component would be:

$$J/P = \left[\left(\frac{J}{N_J}\right)\left(\frac{N_J}{T}\right)\left(\frac{T}{A}\right)\left(\frac{A}{P}\right)\right]$$

Although Canada's Courts do not have adequate data to make the analysis revealing at this point, the value of such a measure is that, with sufficient data, you analyze what mixture of resources provides what level of output. The further microeconomic question is: as the mixture of resources changes, how does that change the output? With reasonable time-series data, we can identify the variety of spending mixes used by the provinces while meeting the demand for judicial attention and trials.

In terms of the court data currently available, it would be very difficult to explore the kind of detailed cost breakdowns described above. What we can describe is the level of costs of the courts and regulatory system in each of the provinces. This invites a natural question: given that there are substantial differences in costs across provinces, is there any reason to believe that the quality of civil justice is different?

Table 9 explores this issue by expressing the real per-capita costs of the court system in each of the provinces as well as nationally. Per-capita is appropriate since larger provinces will spend more than smaller ones, and such a measure suggests the amount of resources per person in the province devoted to maintaining the court system. The figures in the table are adjusted for inflation and expressed in 1994 dollars.

As is apparent from table 11, Canada-wide expenditures on the court system have increased 227 percent in real (*i.e.*, inflation-adjusted dollars) during the past 20 years. The federal component has increased more rapidly than at the provincial level. Among the provinces the real per-capita spending has been greatest in British Columbia, Newfoundland, and in the North West Territories.

Table 11 Real per-capita spending on the court system (1994 dollars)*

	1973–74†	1980–81†	1987–88†	1993–94
Canada	37	60	84	84
Federal	7	14	26	25
Provincial	30	46	58	59
PE	20	38	39	39
NF	17	31	45	49
NS	25	31	53	54
NB	23	28	35	38
PQ	35	49	65	59
ON	32	43	47	46
MB	34	40	53	57
SK	18	43	47	44
AB	27	48	54	52
BC	23	65	86	113‡
YK	93	172	227	211
NT	50	133	217	227

* Source: Paul Reed's *Public Accounts*-based study of Canadian justice expenditures.

† in 1994 Dollars per capita

‡ Although this number for British Columbia seems high, we have had it verified by Dr. Paul Reed.

By 1993/94, court costs in Canada had stabilized nationally although there have been increases in British Columbia and declines in most of the other provinces. The levels, however, vary considerably by province with British Columbia and Quebec spending more than Ontario and the other provinces.

Court delay

Measuring court delay

For the purposes of this discussion, court delay is defined as the time lag between when the demand for a legal service is made and when the suppliers satisfy the demand. In the "real" world, it may be both unnecessary and inefficient for courts to instantaneously provide a trial when a request is made. However, in order to avoid the swamp of subjective interpretations of delay, we start from the assumption that when two parties request a trial, they want one immediately.

Measuring delay is particularly difficult no matter which definition one may choose. Since 1992, the Canadian Judicial Council through its Court Delays Project has sought to survey the extent of delays in superior courts. The challenges they face in doing so are three-fold:

- a lack of standard categories in court registries across the country
- record keeping that ranges from hand written notes to, at best, primitive computer tracking
- institutional resistance to measures that could lead to jurisdictional comparisons and, of course
- scarce resources.

The results, to date, must be applauded but the data on court delay has yet to reach the level and sophistication needed to support critical decisions.

There are only two reliable means to measure delay. The first is to track cases individually through the system. With the possible exception of Manitoba, we are not aware of any province systematically tracking cases in order to gauge delay. The second is to calculate various ratios in the raw year-to-year caseload and trial data. Only a few provinces are likely to have sufficient data to perform such a calculation.

The economics of alternative dispute resolution: the cost of delay

In one sense, it is meaningless to speak about delay and its costs if there is no alternative to the court system. That is, cases may take a subjectively determined "long" time. But, if there is nothing you can do about it, then whatever costs exist, you have to pay. The demand for this service would be inelastic.

Is the demand for formal justice inelastic? The increasing popularity of Alternative/Alternate Dispute Resolution (ADR) suggests that legal consumers are now examining very seriously intermediary methods of dispute resolution that lie between formal court proceedings and simply settling the issue personally with the other party.

In the survey results presented later in this paper, respondents shared the view that ADR had value as a way to shorten the length of disputes and their costs. As to the length of disputes, ADR clearly is attractive. The parties in the case mutually control the timing of the dispute resolution process rather than having to accommodate the timetable of often very busy courts. If ADR wins in the delay category simply by definition, what of costs and the quality of outcomes?

For the sake of this discussion, we will restrict discussion of the relative merits of ADR outcomes and formal court outcomes, to the observation that in some cases we are comparing apples to apples and in others apples to oranges. In other words, ADR may be a substitute for formal court proceedings or it may be a complementary service used to ensure the most efficient use of lawyers and court time. As a substitute, ADR would be "alternative" as in either one or the other. As a complement, ADR would be "alternate" as in a consequential step to formal proceedings.

If the ADR practitioner is replicating even informally the formality of trial logic, then it may be a substitute. Richard Posner and William Landes describe the court system as providing the "public good" of law and doctrine—information arrived at through an intricate and demanding process of inquiry and interpretation commensurate with its importance as a guide to the future decision-making of thousands of people. A retired judge who practices ADR supplies his or her client with an accurate recreation of the logic that would be applied in the formal court process; such a retired judge is providing knowledge of how judges judge. When the judge was on the bench, he or she provided that as a public good;

now it is traded as a private good. To be sure, no retired judge ADR practitioner would claim to know how Judge X will decide a case next month, but rather how all judges might weigh the issues.

In contrast to our example of the retired judge, the ADR practitioner relying on various techniques of arbitration and mediation may instead offer a complementary good to the services already being provided by counsel and the courts. That is, the non-judge mediator assists the parties in reaching a settlement through the compromise of their respective interests rather than a prediction of a legal outcome should they go to trial. That our survey respondents indicated that typically ADR was explained as an alternative to litigation once litigation had already commenced supports the "alternate" view ADR.

Whether the dispute resolution method is "alternative" or "alternate" leads to a different characterization of the costs incurred. The pricing of *Alternative* Dispute Resolution competes directly against the price of formal proceedings. (We have already shown that it competes directly and wins in terms of time to gratification.) The retired judge, for instance, would charge a hefty fee in order that it would be just marginally below that of the fees of a formal court, assuming the courts could provide instantaneous service. The pricing of *Alternate* Dispute Resolution does not compete with the costs of the formal court. They are, instead, additional costs, extra costs entered into in the hope that the service could, in turn, reduce the formal court costs.

The relative price attractiveness of both ADRs is also influenced, though in different ways, by the time it takes to resolve disputes in the formal court process. In other words, the cost of court delay should develop into a factor at the margin of deciding to use or not to use ADR. With alternative ADR, it will be a significant factor because the cost of court delay is fully avoided. With alternate ADR, it is a lesser factor because it is being used only to contain or reduce formal court costs.

To understand how the pricing of ADR might work as a function of the cost of delay, we start with a definition of delay as the gap in immediate gratification of demand. This reductionist characterization allows a simple formula to calculate the cost of delay.

$$CD = \left[\left(\frac{TC}{T} \right) R \ (t_t - t_r) \right]$$

where CD = cost of delay, TC = cost of trials, T = number of trials, R = discount rate, tt = time of trial, and tr = time of trial request.

The cost of delay is the difference between the true cost of a trial (supposing someone was willing to pay for an immediate trial and had to pay the judge's salary, court room costs, and so on) at the time of request, and that same cost increased by the cost of borrowing times the length of time until trial.[14]

To calculate the cost of delay, we first need a rough idea of the time an average case takes from being set down on the trial list to getting into court. For the present calculation, we will use Ontario data because it is one of the few jurisdictions that keeps records on the number of cases added to the trial lists as well as the number of cases pending in each year. In order to get a rough idea of delay, we can calculate the ratio between the number of pending cases and the number of trials. This will give us the system's disposal rate. Obviously, in civil litigation there are a variety of other means of disposal than just by trial (*e.g.*, abandonment) but for the sake of the present discussion we will assume that the only way to work off a pending backlog is by getting the case to trial. The pending cases to trials ratio for Ontario is set out in table 12.

Table 12 Cases and trials in Ontario

	1990/91	1991/92	1992/93	1993/94	1994/95
Pending cases (P)	15,128	25,058	26,187	24,837	21,497
Trials (T)	10,667	9,710	5,549	4,854	4,111
Ratio: P/T	1.4	2.5	4.7	5.1	5.2

Source: Ontario, Ministry of Attorney General, *Court Statistics Annual Report 1994/1995*: 9.

Using Ontario data for 1994/95, we can say that, *at the current disposal rate*, a pending caseload of 21,497 cases would take 5.2 years to work off, assuming all these cases were disposed of by trial. However, this is likely too high a figure for delay, as many of these pending cases will be disposed of without a trial. Taking a more reasonable figure for delay of 10 months,[15] we can proceed to calculate the cost of delay. A case delayed for 10 months at an interest rate of 7.5 percent, means an opportunity cost of $875 to the litigants, assuming that an average court case involves roughly

$14,000[16] worth of resources that are not paid for by the parties themselves. This figure of $875 is an estimate of the cost associated with being denied (for the time period of the delay) access to the public court resources that the parties are going to use to settle the dispute. For a caseload delay of 10 months, in which we have 21,497 cases pending (as is the case in Ontario in 1994/95), we have an aggregate cost to the parties of $875 times 21,497 cases, or $18,809,875. Even if the average case cost to the system is lower, it still suggests a substantial cost to the parties caused by delay, and it helps us to understand some of the concerns of counsel (See survey section).

In our model, the price at which alternate ADR becomes competitive is defined as follows. First, it is the subsidy of the public for a "free trial," an amount of approximately $14,000.[17] (Since this is alternate rather than alternative, the parties have elected to use the public subsidy.) Second, this subsidy is discounted by the average cost of delay to the parties ($875 on average per case). That leaves $13,125. That amount must be netted against the cost to the parties of their legal counsel and other expenses related solely to formal court proceedings. In the following survey, the average case of the respondents cost their organization $22,800. That leaves a difference of $9,675. This, then, is the price that an alternative ADR provider must beat in an average case in Ontario in order to be competitive and attractive to, at least, potential corporate clients who may still see the case through to formal court proceedings.

In the case of the alternative ADR provider, since they are providing a substitute good, the price offered to the client is independent of any anticipated public subsidy. The alternative ADR provider simply has to keep his or her price below the average cost of $22,800.

On balance, the alternative ADR provider has two advantages and one disadvantage in the market for dispute resolution services. He or she has the opportunity for higher pricing before the clients faces a net loss compared to strictly formal proceedings. He or she does not face the pressure that the longer the time to trial, the larger the erosion of the value of the public subsidy, and, therefore, of the value of court-complementary dispute resolution services. The one disadvantage lies in certainty of outcome. If the alternate service provider fails to bring resolution, the concurrent court process will. The client will have only paid a marginal amount in order to bring closure before a formal judgment. If the alternative service provider fails to bring resolution, then the whole court process must begin and the client will have paid twice to resolve the dispute.

User satisfaction: the corporate counsel survey

In this section we present the initial results of the survey sent to 650 members of the Canadian Corporate Counsel Association.[18] The survey asks detailed questions about general and specific experiences with the costs and delays of legal services and their causes. Questions are also asked about counsels use of, and satisfaction with, Alternate Dispute Resolution (ADR) mechanisms. This is a first survey of its kind for Canada. The survey returns were light, with only a 7 percent response rate. Of the surveys, fully 55 percent were from Ontario. Nova Scotia, Price Edward Island, Saskatchewan, and the Territories were not represented.

The survey was divided into two sections. The first explored the general case load of corporate counsels. The second asked counsels to respond to specific questions about a representative case of their choosing. The average values to each of the questions are filled-in to give a sense of the original data.[19]

In the next sections we present an overview of the results of the survey and highlight some of the more interesting observations of corporate counsels.

The case load

In our sample, the corporate counsel dealt with an average of 58 cases each year during the last five years. Most (38 percent) of these cases were about contract law, while 14 percent involved labour or employment issues. Personal injury, product law, and tax matters were the subject of, respectively, 11, 8, and 5 percent of reported cases. Parties to the case were other companies in 46 percent of all cases and individuals in 41 percent of cases. Governments and government agencies at all levels were evenly split and totaled 10 percent of cases. Unions were involved in about 3 percent of cases.

The average counsel who completed the questionnaire began work on the case 10 months after the dispute began. The final disposition took 39 months on average although, if the case went to trial, it took 47 months. Comments by counsel included remarks that "trials: take too long; [and are] too costly;" and that "[t]he plaintiff in this case did nothing to move it forward for, literally, years and there was nothing in the court procedures to prevent that."

The cases were heard in Provincial Superior Trial Court 63 percent of the time and in Provincial Court, 12 percent of the time. Tribunals heard 9 percent of the cases and provincial Appeals Court heard another 6 percent of all cases. About 10 percent were heard in other courts.

Of those cases that were disposed of during the last five years, 54 percent were settled without going to court or using ADR (alternative disputes resolution.) Some 12 percent were resolved by pre-trial conference, 11 percent were withdrawn or abandoned, while 4 percent were resolved by arbitration and 3 percent by ADR. In our sample, fifteen percent of all cases were settled by trial. Some 70 percent of the respondents were satisfied or very satisfied with the outcome of the case.

The average case took 223 hours of counsel time and was estimated to have cost the organization $22,800. Other in-house costs were 52 hours with additional costs of $7,300 dollars. Outside counsel were paid $101,860 on average in the cases reported and disbursements added another $9,260. Experts were hired for an average of $9,000 with additional costs of $570, while court fees and transcripts amounted to an average of $3,770. Management and staff spent some 225 hours on this case and this cost $17,700. All of these meant that on average some 387 hours and $106,100 were spent on this representative case.[20] Let us put this in context. The average sales of a company responding to this survey were $995 million with 3,862 employees.[21] The cost of the average number of cases (58) is $6.2 million or one-half of one percent of sales.[22]

Case characterization

The cases themselves were considered "complex" or "very complex" 70 percent of the time. "Factual complexity," followed by "the number and complexity of the legal issues," and "the complexity of technical evidence" were the most significant contributors to the counsel's account of the causes of complexity. Less important causes were "the number of witnesses" (lay or expert), "the complexity of procedures," or "the number of parties."

Counsel considered most cases to have been "long" or "too long." The reasons are first, "actions (or inaction) by other parties and their lawyers"; and, second, "too much (civil) backlog in the courts." These results, however, are heavily weighted by the Ontario respondents who comprised 50 percent of our sample. Although this is clearly an issue in Ontario, there may be a backlog problem in other provinces, but we do not have enough statistical information to form any conclusion. Anecdotally, Quebec, Ontario, and British Columbia have similar backlog problems.

The "length and complexity of the issues," "oral discoveries," and "court management and scheduling" were identified as among the more significant of the reasons for delay. Other possible reasons that do not appear to be too important include behaviour by one's own lawyers or management, the "court rules or procedures," "time spent at case management meetings," and "the number of pretrial motions." Criminal caseload backlog was not cited as a significant cause of delay.

In terms of choosing trial court dates, 27 percent were satisfied or very satisfied with the time to availability, and 36 percent were "somewhat dissatisfied" or "very dissatisfied." Among the reasons given for dissatisfaction were that scheduling led to excessive length and did not take into account the needs of the parties for speed of resolution. For appeals and interlocutory matters there was little that stood out as creating dissatisfaction.

The role of outside counsel was seen as very positive. They were generally seen as "efficient," "competent," and "effective." Opinion was equally split on whether they were "reasonably paid" or "overpaid."

The costs of litigation were characterized as "about right" in one-third of all cases. One-quarter of all respondents thought they were "high," and 40 percent thought they were either "too high" or "far too high" in the typical case they chose for the survey.

Counsel said that the most important factor leading to higher costs was that "the amount at stake was too high not to pursue the action." The "complexity of the factual material and legal issues," the behaviour of the other parties and their lawyers, as well as legal fees, were all seen as significant contributors to costs. Court management and scheduling, delays caused by backlogs in court, and the complexity of documents also had a role to play.

Case management and ADR

Case management analysis reveals that in most cases judges were seen as playing a low or minimal role in managing the case.

Had the judge played more of a role, counsel felt that the time to disposition would have been reduced significantly, although it was not thought that it would have reduced costs to their company in an important way.

Of those who went to litigation, about one-third had outside counsel explain the ADR options that were available. In a quarter of the cases in which ADR options were not explained, counsel felt that such an explanation would have made a difference in their decision to proceed to trial or litigation. Typically, ADR was explained as an alternative to litigation once litigation had been commenced, rather than before litigating or as an adjunct to litigation. This timing was not seen as important to the decision to litigate. Only about 13 percent of our sample used ADR, so it was not possible to obtain useful information about the ADR process itself.

For those who did not use ADR, *most* felt that ADR would have given the same results for the same costs and would have taken the same amount of time. Many also felt that the issues in the case were not amenable to ADR-type resolution. In addition, some of those who did not use ADR cited a refusal on the part of the other party to consider ADR options as a principal reason for not using ADR. One-third of those who did not use ADR thought that it should have been used. Of these, most believed that the use of ADR would have reduced the time to disposition and the cost of the case to their corporation

Conclusion

At present around $11 billion is spent on civil justice in Canada. Despite the size and importance of this market, the evidence about such simple basic matters as the caseload and its disposition, let alone the resources used in case management and resolution, is remarkably sparse. It is simply too early to form any hard and fast conclusions about the civil justice system in Canada. After nearly two years of research at The Fraser Institute, we are just now beginning to have enough data to "guess-timate" simply the number of trials in Canada let alone the sum of money passing hands in Canadian court rooms. The rule with justice statistics is "if you can ask the question, no one has the numbers."

This lack of information ought to be addressed. Our first of a kind survey evidence reveals dissatisfaction among practitioners with delay and case management in particular jurisdictions. The costs from an aggregate perspective are substantial and affect economic activity. There are also significant cost differences among the provinces, and it is still an open issue whether these are because of differences in general economic activity, cost efficiency in dealing with civil cases, or more subtle differences in case load and mix.

Why does this matter? A simple enough reason is that, despite a rigorous empirical point of reference, efforts at legal reform steam forward. To be sure, attitudes towards numbers have changed. Certainly the Ontario Civil Justice Review deserves substantial credit in starting to appreciate the value of such a perspective. Yet, the risks to the system and to the economy, as a whole, remain substantial without some extensive understanding of the economics of the justice system. To understand the potential consequences of such risky behavior one only has to look south of the border.

Richard Epstein in his 1995 book, *Simple Rules for a Complex World*, describes a bell-shaped curve representing the supply of law and lawyers plotted against their economic contribution. His thesis is that the United States has passed the peak, perhaps by as much as 40 percent, and that there currently exist "too many lawyers, too much law." As a result, the law has come to distort economic incentives, producing unintended harmful consequences. He calls for a "fresh start" through a re-invigoration of the "simple rules" of the common law and a retrenchment of the social ambitions of the state. If achieved, the legal system could once again serve to increase the efficiency of economic markets in creating wealth.

Canada has not gone as far along Epstein's curve as has the United States. Walter Olson of the Manhattan Institute opines that Canada is ten years behind. Yet, the conditions exist for Canada to catch up swiftly to the United States in the progression of its own legal arteriosclerosis. *Class action* suits are now permitted in Quebec, Ontario, and British Columbia. Law schools keep churning out more bright young lawyers who, if they are to survive, must aggressively seek new business—read, new victims of corporate and government negligence. Informal *contingency fees* have already begun to finance previously marginal legal actions. Governments continue to enact ever more detailed *laws* and *regulations*, while ignoring their impact on an already clogged court system and on the tightened profits of Canadian businesses.

It is one thing to claim that Canada's economic efficiency will suffer if current legal trends continue. It is quite another to prove it. You need evidence to show how and why economic loss might happen, and to suggest ways to correct the trajectory. Epstein admits that even in the United States there are only "some early returns" in the empirical measurement and analysis of the law and legal system's effect on productivity. (Texas Professor Stephen Magee, in a *Wall Street Journal* piece, estimated that each additional lawyer in the United States reduces the level of GDP by $2.5 million.)

It may sound hyperbolic considering we are talking about "dull" court statistics. It may be true there are lies, damn lies, and statistics. But, they are fundamental building blocks necessary to understand the interaction of law, the justice system, and the economy in Canada.

Acknowledgments

This paper is a revision of that presented to the Canadian Bar Association's Task Force on Civil Justice, February, 1996. We have benefited from many comments and would like to thank David Tavender in particular for his suggestions.

Notes

1 One caveat we have is that Statistics Canada does not separate civil from criminal legal services in its survey. For a category like accommodation this is not an important distinction, but for a category like *legal services not elsewhere specified*, some are probably related to criminal legal services although the bulk are most likely to be related to family and vehicle expenses. In our research we have always separated criminal from civil legal spending. We have not been able to do so in the consumer spending category, but we imagine most consumer spending on legal services is not related to criminal matters. With our estimates of court expenditures, we have apportioned costs between civil and criminal using a *pro rata* share based on number of

court hours devoted to each activity. It is an appalling feature of Canadian judicial financial accountability that it is not possible to state without ambiguity what fraction of both the case load and of court expenditures is due to civil rather than criminal matters. As is discussed below, among other suggestions we strongly recommend that data be collected that permit this obviously important characterisation of the legal system to be observed.

2 Although this is nominally an identity, we have been at pains to point out that the data have not been reconciled. We have estimates of expenditures and receipts that arise from different sources.

3 Consumer spending for legal services associated with accommodation tends to be more volatile than other consumer spending. In the 1992 survey, spending on accommodation was about 56 percent of the spending category described in the table. However accommodation related legal services spending has varied from equality to 35 percent of non-accommodation related spending.

4 It is important to acknowledge the distinction between civil legal spending and spending on the resolution of civil disputes. The latter is a much larger category including regulation of uncontentious matters. Our analysis picks up what surveys identify as legal spending on civil matters and on what is reported in the public accounts as related to spending on regulatory bodies and civil justice. Some spending on civil legal matters is clearly involved in avoiding litigation. Furthermore, as we will see below in table 7, there are fewer actions being filed now than in the recent past. But the broad point remains, there is increasing spending on legal services.

5 We are, of course, aware that not all business legal spending is for dispute resolution. Although the corporate counsel survey emphasizes litigation costs, the use of all legal firm income less that accounted for by government and consumer spending on legal services helps us capture more than simply dispute resolution.

6 As they stand, the values for business spending in tables 1 and 3 are correct with respect to the rates of change but assume a constant fraction of in-house spending relative to contracted-out spending.

7 This court data has been gathered from provincial annual reports as well as by special requests for data made to provincial court statisticians. Some provinces keep data on both the number of initial filings as well as the number of trials; some, however, only keep a record of the initial filings' count. Only Ontario produces any data on trial list activity, e.g. pending lists, number of cases disposed of per annum. Manitoba, Newfoundland, Nova Scotia, and the Yukon do not track the number of civil trials they hold in their provincial superior trial courts. We have been unable to obtain any information caseload statistics from Prince Edward Island.

8 On May 28, 1990 mandatory no-fault automobile insurance was introduced in Ontario.

9 For our figures on court expenditures we have used the *Public Accounts*-based measurement provided by Dr. Paul Reed of Statistics Canada.

10 It should be stressed that this figure is only the marginal cost of running the courts; it represents the cost of running an additional trial; it does not include the fixed cost of building another court house, let alone the cost of constructing a whole new justice system.

11 For a representative example see James S. Kakalik and Abby E. Robyn, *Costs of the Civil Justice System: Court Expenditures for Processing Tort Cases*. Santa Monica, CA: Rand Corporation Institute for Civil Justice, 1982.

12 They do not take into account any revenues generated by the court system.

13 For example, the equation for the salary cost per trial would be as follows:

$$(T\hat{C}/T) = \theta_L(\hat{s}_L + \hat{N}_L - \hat{T}) + \theta_J(\hat{s}_J + \hat{N}_J - \hat{T}) + \theta_R(\hat{R} - \hat{T})$$

14 Alternatively, we could take the difference between the value of the public resources used on a trial taking place today, and the value of those (present) resources when delivered in the future.

15 The figure of 10 months for Ontario comes from the Trial Courts Committee of the Canadian Judicial Council (1995).

16 The figure of $14,000 is taken from our calculation of the cost to the system of a superior court civil trial in Ontario (see page 13 above). We have rounded this figure down for ease of calculation.

17 This, of course, does not include the cost to the parties of their own counsel. If anything, the private cost of litigation is likely to be higher than the cost of the public subsidy. (The Ontario Civil Justice Review (1995): 144, estimates that for a three day trial, the cost to the litigants would be roughly $38,000). We are assuming that parties value the court services at cost, although demand theory suggests that since the services are priced at (nearly) zero to the participants, they will be overused and valued at less than the cost of provision.

18 We are particularly grateful to the Canadian Corporate Counsel Association for helping us garner a picture of corporate litigation in Canada. This kind of basic research is fundamental to understanding Canada's legal system, and we recognize that it imposes a cost on the participants who voluntarily make the effort. Both the Canadian Bar Association and the CCCA have been very helpful in developing the questionnaire, and we gratefully acknowledge their insights and assistance. We must emphasize that neither are responsible for the interpretation we present.

19 In most cases, averages are reported. In some cases, the questions are blank as not enough replies were obtained to interpret the question meaningfully. Percentages of responses are reported where relevant, rather than absolute counts, in order to facilitate interpretation and comparison.

20 The reason the average case cost is less than the sum of the in-house, external counsel, experts costs, etc. is that different cases involve a different mix of requirements. In the survey, we did not require counsel to make sure the sums added-up. The overall figure is more likely to be a reliable one in any case as it was answered by more respondents some of whom did not break down their expenses into the various categories mentioned in the text.

21 The average size of company is clearly very large. It represents a few very large corporations and many smaller ones. If the final sample is sufficiently large, we can break out the very large from the more numerous smaller companies.

22 This is not an outrageous figure. Canada spent roughly $12 billion on civil legal services. Since GDP is about $750 billion, the corporate component of legal services is clearly the same order of magnitude reflected in the survey —around 0.5 percent of sales.